Power Sharing and I
in Ethnic Conflicts

Power Sharing and International Mediation in Ethnic Conflicts

TIMOTHY D. SISK

CARNEGIE COMMISSION ON
PREVENTING DEADLY CONFLICT
CARNEGIE CORPORATION OF NEW YORK

United States Institute of Peace
Washington, D.C.

United States Institute of Peace
1550 M Street NW, Suite 700
Washington, DC 20005-1708

Carnegie Commission on Preventing Deadly Conflict
2400 N Street NW, Sixth Floor
Washington, DC 20037-1153

First published 1996

Printed in the United States of America

The paper used in this publication meets the minimum requirements of American National Standard for Information Sciences—Permanence of Paper for Printed Library Materials, ANSI Z39.48-1984.

Library of Congress Cataloging-in-Publication Data
Sisk, Timothy D., 1960–
     Power sharing and international mediation in ethnic conflicts /
     Timothy D. Sisk.
        p. cm. — (Perspectives series)
     Includes bibliographical references.
     ISBN 1-878379-56-9
     1. Ethnic groups—Political activity. 2. Minorities—Political activity.
     3. Democracy. 4. Representative government and representation.
     I. Title. II. Series.
JF1061.S57 1996
322.4'4'08693—dc20   96-8127
                                                                   CIP

Contents

Summary

Despite the proliferation of newly independent states in the Cold War's immediate aftermath, many of which were once in the former Soviet Union, most ethnic group claims to self-determination are unlikely to be realized if this principle is defined as a separate fully sovereign state for each ethnic group. For a variety of reasons, the dissolution of existing multiethnic states into new, ethnically homogeneous countries is fraught with problems, evidenced by the reality that much blood has been spilled in recent years in the pursuit of this often elusive goal.

Moreover, given increasing emphasis on democratic governance as a fundamental human right, ethnic group claims for self-determination should ideally be accommodated in a democratic framework *within* existing states. Although not all ethnic conflicts begin as a quest for territorial sovereignty and self-determination, they often result in such maximalist claims unless they are addressed early and effectively. Power sharing, defined as practices and institutions that result in broad-based governing coalitions generally inclusive of all major ethnic groups in society, can reconcile principles of self-determination and democracy in multiethnic states, principles that are often perceived to be at odds.

Although power sharing normally evolves out of internal processes, the international community as an external player has often sought to promote power sharing in response to ethnic conflicts. There have been some successes and some failures; some pitfalls have been avoided and others have not. Rarely is the international community's promotion of power sharing informed by a thorough understanding of the leading contemporary scholarship on the issue. A more systematic appreciation of the scholarly analysis of power sharing can highlight the advantages and disadvantages of various approaches and practices for the amelioration of ethnic conflict.

This book presents the scholarly and practitioner debate over power sharing in the context of ethnic conflict dynamics and identifies the principal approaches to, and practices of, power sharing. It also highlights concerns and problems with power-sharing approaches and practices that have been raised by scholars and practitioners alike, and instances where power-sharing experiments failed. In conclusion, it raises issues regarding international intervention in ethnic conflicts to promote power sharing as a means to prevent or manage violent conflicts in societies deeply divided by ethnic differences. This summary highlights some key points.

Ethnic Conflict: Approaches, Patterns, and Dynamics

- Ethnic conflict is explained by scholars as either primordial and innate, or instrumental and (at least partially) socially contrived. The extent to which analysts perceive ethnicity as immutable and innate versus socially constructed or manipulated by political leaders influences beliefs about the types of institutions and practices that can best ameliorate conflict along ethnic lines. A critical factor is whether ethnic groups perceive each other in essentialist, threatening terms, or pragmatically. Pragmatic perceptions between groups in conflict create opportunities for peaceful management of intergroup relations.

- Ethnic conflicts can be more or less severe, depending in large part on the structure of relationships, for example, whether identity and socioeconomic differences overlap. An important predictor of the severity of conflict is the role of the state: Does it stand above conflicts and mediate them, or does a group "own" the state and use its powers to the detriment of other groups?

- A common thread that runs through all violent ethnic conflicts is the manipulative role of ethnic group leaders who foster discrimination and mobilize group members against their foes. Ethnic *outbidding* refers to extremist ethnic group leaders who decry moderation with enemies as a sellout of group interests.

- Ethnic conflicts can escalate—that is, intensify or spread—or they can de-escalate, resulting in improved intergroup relations. The post–Cold War world contains examples of both. Escalation occurs when background conditions of ethnic strife are combined with *conflict triggers*, or precipitating events. A useful way to conceptualize moves toward more peaceful ethnic conflict management is through a phases or stages approach to de-escalation, in which conflicts that reach a stalemate are managed through protracted negotiations.

Democracy and Its Alternatives in Deeply Divided Societies

- Ethnic conflicts have usually been managed with nondemocratic, authoritarian practices such as subjugation and control. However, informal practices of ethnic balancing have at times kept a relative peace even in societies that are not democratic. Democracy is inherently difficult in divided societies, but democratic practices offer greater promise for long-term peaceful conflict management than nondemocratic ones. Even when democracy is unlikely to be introduced quickly in a society, practices can be put in place that help manage ethnic tensions.

- Simple majoritarian democracy contains special problems for ethnically divided societies. Minority ethnic groups expect to be permanently excluded from power through the ballot box and fear electoral contests when the principle of simple majority rule is operative. Power-sharing practices offer an alternative to simple majoritarian practices of democratic governance.

- There are two broad approaches to constructing democracy in divided societies: the *consociational*, or group building-block, approach that relies on accommodation by ethnic group leaders at the center and a high degree of group autonomy; and the *integrative* approach, which seeks to create incentives for moderation by political leaders on divisive ethnic themes and to enhance minority influence in majority decision making. Consociational approaches rely on elite accommodation and guarantees to groups to protect their interests, such as a mutual or minority veto, whereas the integrative approach relies on incentives for intergroup cooperation such as electoral systems that encourage the formation of preelection pacts among candidates or political parties across ethnic lines. This book argues that both approaches can lead to power sharing while acknowledging that there is some debate about whether the term applies to integrative practices as well.

A Typology of Conflict-Regulating Practices

- The consociational and integrative approaches can be fruitfully viewed as conceptual poles in a spectrum of specific conflict-regulating institutions and practices that promote power sharing. Which approach and which practices are best in any given conflict situation is highly contingent on the patterns and dynamics of the particular conflict. Indeed, a given political system may fruitfully incorporate aspects of both approaches simultaneously. It is useful to consider the practices in terms of three sets of variables that apply to both approaches: territorial division of power, decision rules, and public policies (for example, on language, education, and resource distribution) that define relations between the state and the ethnic groups.
- Five consociational conflict-regulating practices are as follows:
  1. Granting territorial autonomy and creating confederal arrangements.
  2. Creating a polycommunal, or ethnic, federation.
  3. Adopting group proportional representation in administrative appointments, including consensus decision rules in the executive.
  4. Adopting a highly proportional electoral system in a parliamentary framework.
  5. Acknowledging group rights or corporate (nonterritorial) federalism.

- Five integrative conflict-regulating practices are as follows:
  1. Creating a mixed, or nonethnic, federal structure.
  2. Establishing an inclusive, centralized unitary state.
  3. Adopting majoritarian but ethnically neutral, or nonethnic, executive, legislative, and administrative decision-making bodies.
  4. Adopting a semimajoritarian or semiproportional electoral system that encourages the formation of preelection coalitions (vote pooling) across ethnic divides.
  5. Devising "ethnicity-blind" public policies.

Power Sharing and Peace Processes

- Power-sharing practices, when they are adopted by parties in conflicts, often evolve in direct response to a history of violent conflict. Pragmatic perceptions toward other groups can emerge from the belief that the failure to accommodate will precipitate wider strife; political leaders and publics must be motivated to avoid worsening or more violent conflict if power sharing is to be successfully adopted. Unfortunately, such motivation does not always exist: high levels of violence do not inevitably mean that political leaders will be more moderate and adopt power sharing.
- Transitional moments, both in terms of changes in structure of international relations and in terms of relations among groups within states, are moments of promise and peril. Ethnic relations can improve or worsen. Power sharing can evolve from transitions or peace processes in which parties adopt agreements, or *mutual security pacts*, that seek to limit the ability of groups to inflict mutual harm. The degree of unity and organizational coherence of the parties, and the ability of political leaders to persuade their constituents to act peacefully, are the most important variables in creating improved relations among ethnic groups. Conciliatory attitudes must be both broad (including hard-liners) and deep (including key publics as well as leaders).

International Intervention and Power Sharing

- International intervention in ethnic conflicts focuses both on the process by which groups rearrange their relations, through violence or dialogue, and on the terms and structures of the outcomes that are reached. Despite the inherent problems of partition, the international community should not assume that the borders of an existing state are sacrosanct. The principal decision the international community must face in any given violent ethnic conflict is whether separation or power sharing (living together) is the more achievable, sustainable, and just outcome. This is especially true when the parties themselves cannot reach an agreement on this fundamental question.

- The international community often places too much emphasis on democratic elections without considering their potentially adverse impact in situations of severe ethnic conflict, especially when such elections are held with simple majority rule electoral systems and without prior mutual security pacts. Elections are critical moments in peace processes; they are turning points at which relations can polarize or new national unity can be forged through the creation of a legitimate government. Much depends on both the electoral system chosen and the administration and monitoring of the election event. Elections provide important opportunities for intervention to help ameliorate ethnic conflicts because they are especially amenable to monitoring and an ongoing international presence.

- Both historically and more recently, the international community has promoted power sharing by offering formulas—institutional blueprints for postconflict political structures—and has often sought to induce disputants to accept them through a combination of diplomatic carrots and sticks. Increasingly, the international community is using linkages to other issues, such as membership in collective security, trade, and other international organizations, to induce states to adopt practices that promote ethnic accommodation. Promoting conflict-regulating practices in this manner can be a useful tool of preventive diplomacy to arrest the potential escalation of ethnic conflicts into violence.

- The paradox of promoting power sharing *early* in the escalation of an ethnic conflict is that at a nascent stage of tensions, parties may be unwilling to embrace power-sharing practices because they are not sufficiently desperate or feel insufficiently compelled. At a *late* stage of conflict, after significant violence, enmities may be too deep for parties to share power for mutual benefit. Determining when a conflict is ripe for a power-sharing solution is at best a difficult judgment call requiring intimate knowledge of a situation, especially of the true predisposition of the parties and their willingness to live together within a common or shared political framework.

- Thus, a second paradox is the problem of judging intentions. Tactical adoption of power sharing can set the stage for new grievances and new strife. Moreover, the international community is often asked to secure successful implementation of agreements or to guarantee them, which in essence ties the international community to the substance of a settlement.

- The promotion of power sharing by the international community in situations of deep ethnic conflict is riddled with normative considerations, such as potentially rewarding aggression or appeasement of extremists. It also entails considerable risks, such as inducing parties to share power when their underlying perceptions are still deeply suspicious and based on mutual harm.

- When an international mediator goes beyond facilitating negotiation and backs a power-sharing solution in any given conflict at either an early or late stage of escalation, this policy involves choosing sides. This is true of choosing among parties to a conflict (often in favor of minorities who seek to limit the power of majorities) as well as bolstering more moderate factions within a given party or government against more hard-line elements.

Policy Making and Power Sharing

- Power sharing involves a wide range of practices, not a simple model or formula that can be universally applied. Thus, in a given conflict there is no substitute for intimate scholarly and policymaker knowledge in reaching conclusions about whether any given power-sharing practice will likely have an ameliorative or potentially adverse effect on a given ethnic conflict. For example, in some situations consociational power sharing may be an appropriate interim measure but should not become a permanent feature of political life. Likewise, parties in an ethnic conflict may be too insecure to accept the incentive mechanisms of the integrative approach, preferring the more firm guarantees of consociationalism.

- In many countries, democracy may be a long way off, but the international community can exert pressure for the adoption of conflict-regulating practices by nondemocratic states, such as fair treatment of ethnic minorities and ethnically diverse security forces.

- Conditional generalizations can be made that can serve to inform policy. Power-sharing arrangements are successful in managing ethnic conflict under the following conditions:

  1. They are embraced by a core group of moderate political leaders in ethnic conflicts and these leaders are genuinely representative of the groups they purport to lead.

  2. The practices are flexible and allow for equitable distribution of resources.

  3. They are indigenously arrived at, not agreed on as the result of too-heavy external pressures or short-term, zero-sum expectations of the parties.

  4. Parties can gradually eschew the extraordinary measures that some power-sharing practices entail and allow a more integrative and liberal form of democracy to evolve.

Foreword

The horrors of ethnic violence defy imagination: mass murder, rape, and wanton destruction of places of worship and universities carried out by people who had lived together peacefully. The world watches, seemingly helpless before the overwhelming force of hatred, and asks the inevitable question: "Couldn't someone have done something to prevent this?"

People who have devoted their lives to the study of ethnic conflict have sought answers to three components of this large question. What political conditions drive people to violence? What circumstances allow people to settle their differences peacefully? What is the role of the international community when relations between groups become violent or threaten to become violent? Scholars have developed theories of ethnic conflict and of political institutions that can manage conflicts to prevent them from turning violent. They have extracted principles from detailed research on past conflicts, and situations in which conflicts have been avoided, and they have presented their results to policymakers, hoping that the principles will help guide foreign policy.

But scholars notice that policymakers' eyes often glaze over in response to scholarly analyses. The scholar and policymaker are from two different cultures and thrive on different types of information. The scholar looks backward to find lessons; the policymaker looks ahead and adapts to uncertain circumstances. The scholar can wait until all the facts are in; the policymaker must improvise. The time horizon of the scholar may be years; the horizon of the policymaker is often weeks, days, or hours. Scholars complain that policymakers' decisions are ad hoc and without a strategy informed by thoughtful analysis. Policymakers say that they often have no choice but to formulate operational policies by instinct.

In Timothy Sisk's pathbreaking study of power sharing, copublished by the Carnegie Commission on Preventing Deadly Conflict and the United States Institute of Peace, scholarship bridges the gap to policymaking. This is a highly innovative study that applies theories of democracy in multiethnic societies to international mediation aimed at preventing or ameliorating ethnic violence.

As Sisk notes, in deeply divided societies, where fear and ignorance are the driving forces of ethnic conflict, people tend to identify themselves by their ethnic group, the defining characteristic of social order. Violence can erupt in such societies, especially when there is gross inequality among ethnic groups and discrimination against one or more groups, and when discrimination is reinforced by public policy. To avoid such violence, political institutions must allow ethnic groups to participate in the political process and they must protect human rights. Only in such circumstances will ethnic groups be likely to feel valued.

The power-sharing arrangements described in this book can lead divided societies toward stable democracy and away from violence. Power sharing, appropriately structured, can encourage moderation and discourage extremism—and it can be based on politicians' self-interest: They will do what is needed to get elected. Power sharing can initiate the profound movement of a society away from ethnicity as the strongest social identifier. Coalitions may form along ethnic lines at the outset, but ideology or class may become more important in time. Such a shift may be helpful, as people feel strongly about ideology and class, but they are less likely to fight to the death for these values than ethnic extremists.

Power sharing has been successful in some societies but ineffective in others. It was essential in the peaceful change of government in South Africa. Without an agreement on transitional power sharing, the conflict over apartheid might not have been brought to an end, or a new round of killing might have occurred. Yet a power-sharing pact in Rwanda did not prevent genocide. For this reason, the book focuses on the conditions under which the international community should promote power-sharing efforts to prevent deadly conflict.

The lessons of this work are highly relevant for the leaders of deeply divided societies and for the international community attempting to prevent ethnic conflicts. All too often, international mediation deals only with the *process* of political change: Is it going to be peaceful or violent? Mediators want to prevent or stop the violence by any means possible. The international community must be more involved in shaping the *institutions* that will ensure an enduring peace—the *outcomes* of political change. Mediation needs to be invoked early on and address what may be the most important question: Is power sharing necessary, and possible, in a given society—or is separation a better course? Prescriptions are not possible because every situation has its unique aspects. The value of this book is in the range of options presented to policymakers as well as the illumination of critical issues.

Sisk's study draws on the experience of a number of Institute of Peace activities and initiatives on peacemaking in multiethnic societies. In addition to numerous Institute-funded grant and fellowship projects on specific conflicts, many in-house activities in recent years have focused on ethnic conflict amelioration, with special emphasis on the former Yugoslavia, Africa, the former Soviet Union, and South Asia. For example, one of the Institute's earliest grants supported the volume edited by Joseph Montville, *Conflict and Peacemaking in Multiethnic Societies*, upon which the Sisk book builds. The Institute has also focused on the tools of conflict prevention, work which yielded the recently published Institute Press book *Preventing Violent Conflicts: A Strategy for Preventive Diplomacy*, by Michael Lund.

A wide array of past and present Institute programs on religion and conflict, the rule of law and transitional justice, negotiation and mediation, elections and conflict resolution, and managing today's "complex humanitarian emergencies" through peacekeeping and diplomacy also relate to the power-sharing theme.

The Carnegie Commission on Preventing Deadly Conflict is deeply concerned with the democratic processes that Sisk describes. In identifying preventive measures, the Commission distinguishes between long-term structural tasks and immediate operational tasks to defuse a crisis. Structural prevention includes strategies to build intercommunal confidence, overcome deeply held mistrust, and restructure institutions that discriminate against certain ethnic groups. Democratization, which performs all these tasks, is a crucial element of structural prevention. Thus the Commission supports research—such as this work—and international fora to highlight the role that democratic institutions and power-sharing arrangements must play in the post–Cold War world. A study by Larry Diamond, a leading scholar of democratization, led to a recent Commission report, *Promoting Democracy in the 1990s: Actors and Instruments, Issues and Imperatives.* An upcoming forum in Moscow will address power sharing among institutions, minority groups, and the states of the former Soviet Union. The established democracies, with so much relevant experience, can play essential catalyzing and sustaining roles to help countries negotiate the complicated and slow process of democratization. The Commission is attempting to distill lessons from the recent record of the international community in conflict prevention.

Ethnic conflicts will continue to be a challenging aspect of the post–Cold War world. And many of these conflicts could easily become very violent. The critical question is whether pre-conflict situations can be managed to prevent the turn to violence, ideally through the structures of participatory democracy. An alert, active international community—with the close collaboration of scholars and policymakers—can help contending parties forestall violence by encouraging the adoption of an appropriately structured power-sharing agreement based on democratic principles.

We hope that this book, a road map to scholarship and analysis of the role of the international community in promoting ethnic amity, will serve the policy and academic communities well as they grapple with today's—and tomorrow's—conflicts.

David A. Hamburg, Cochair
Carnegie Commission on Preventing Deadly Conflict

Richard H. Solomon, President
United States Institute of Peace

Preface

This book has its origins in a previous book by the author on the negotiated transition from apartheid to inclusive, nonracial democracy in South Africa (*Democratization in South Africa: The Elusive Social Contract*, Princeton University Press). Those concerned with the amelioration of ethnic conflict in the post–Cold War era turn to the South African experience for lessons learned that may be applicable to other countries. Power sharing, it is widely believed, was an appropriate transitional outcome to the South African negotiations because it allowed for a careful balancing of majority prerogatives and minority interests in the immediate post-apartheid era. Without power sharing, the white minority may have sought to fight enfranchisement of the black majority to the bitter end.

The international community played an important role in fostering relatively peaceful change in South Africa ("relatively" peaceful because some 14,000 people died in political violence during the transition period), even if the decision to create a five-year government of national unity after apartheid was an internal one. External mediation did occur in South Africa, but it was either indirect or last-minute. External intervention to end apartheid, however, was extensive and sustained for many decades. The international community made a difference in South Africa, even if the conflict was transformed at a late stage, after much suffering and bloodshed.

Can *early* promotion of power sharing by the international community stave off violent ethnic conflict? If so, when, if, and how? The intent of this book is to begin to shed some light on these questions.

The study of power sharing has previously been the domain of students of comparative politics, while the issues of mediation and intervention are studied by students of international relations. This book seeks to bring these two strands of scholarship together in an effort to promote greater understanding of the possibilities and pitfalls of intervention to pre-empt the deterioration of ethnic relations into violence through the early and appropriate adoption of power-sharing institutions and practices.

The author thanks the Carnegie Commission on Preventing Deadly Conflict for its support of this work, and for the intellectual guidance provided by commission member Alexander I. George and executive director Jane E. Holl, along with the excellent staff work of senior associate Tom Leney and administrative/research assistant Nancy Ward.

The author also thanks the following individuals for their thorough and thoughtful comments on an earlier draft of this book: Steven L. Burg of Brandeis University; Pierre du Toit of the University of Stellenbosch (South Africa); Milton Esman of Cornell University; Donald L. Horowitz of Duke University; Arend Lijphart of the University of California, San Diego; Donald Rothchild of the University of California, Davis; Ambassador Herbert S. Okun, special advisor to the commission; and Andrew S. Reynolds of the University of California, San Diego. Initial research assistance was provided by Chuck Call of Stanford University in addition to the sharing of his own fine research into Colombia's National Front, cited in the text. Thanks to Nils Petter Gleditsch of the Peace Research Institute, Oslo, for the opportunity to present this research to the working group on ethnic conflict that he coordinates there.

Acknowledgments and thanks are also due to the United States Institute of Peace, for encouraging and allowing this contribution to the Carnegie Commission's work, and to the Norwegian Nobel Institute, Oslo, Norway, at which the author was a visiting researcher while revisions to the manuscript were made. Comments and suggestions from the Nobel Institute's director, Geir Lundestad, and director of research, Odd Arne Westad, helped the author refine his ideas on several critical topics.

Power Sharing and International Mediation in Ethnic Conflicts

1

Introduction

"Self-determination" is the rallying cry of many aggrieved ethnic groups in every major region of the world.[1] In 1992, a study by the Carnegie Endowment for International Peace identified more than sixty states with active subnational movements seeking self-determination: either their own sovereign state or a significant measure of minority (or majority) rights (Halperin, Scheffer, and Small 1992:123–157).[2] More than ever before, the lure of a homogeneous nation-state—our country for our nation—is viewed by many ethnic groups as an answer to their inability to coexist with others in a common state.

Most ethnic groups seeking to manifest their claims for self-determination through the creation of ethnically homogeneous nation-states will not be successful. U.S. political scientist Samuel Huntington has written that "the twentieth century bias against political divorce, that is, secession, is just about as strong as the nineteenth century bias against marital divorce."[3] When ethnic groups with deep enmities "can't go on living together," he adds, "they go on living together. They have no choice" (Huntington 1972:i).

Times have changed since Huntington penned his remarks; rightly or wrongly, aggrieved ethnic groups now perceive the creation of new sovereign states to give life to the principle of self-determination as an achievable alternative. Independence for the former Soviet republics, the breakup of the former Yugoslavia into five new states, the bifurcation of the former Czechoslovakia, and the successful Eritrean struggle to separate from Ethiopia have given new impetus to those seeking an ethnic state. The depth of enmity in ethnic conflicts has also provoked reconsideration of the virtues of territorial integrity of states such as Sudan or Rwanda, where some observers have reached the conclusion that peaceful coexistence within the existing country will never be possible.

The bias against secession in international law and practice remains strong. The principle of self-determination, enshrined in Article 1.2 of the United Nations Charter, is still *not* equated in international law and practice with the blanket right of an aggrieved ethnic group to a separate sovereign state, as Max Kampelman has adroitly argued (1993).[4] The determination of the international community to maintain the territorial integrity of Bosnia and Herzegovina, despite the brutality of the civil war among its three principal communities, attests to this fact.

Moreover, where secession has occurred, the new states invariably contain their own minorities; partition does not *solve* problems of multiethnic coexistence, it only rearranges the configuration of minorities and majorities. Although the newly independent states of the former Soviet Union carry ethnic names, all have their own minorities. In occurrences of partition, such as the violent dissolution of British India and the creation of Pakistan in 1947, the enmities generated by separation can continue for generations; formerly internal conflicts may be transformed to international conflicts but certainly are not resolved. In India and Pakistan today, the fruits of partition are doggedly persistent internal political violence and bitter and dangerous discord between the countries.

Although the bias against secession remains strong, disputants and the international community alike face a fundamental choice: allow partition and political divorce, or create new more viable structures for living together in a common polity. Until there is a significant change in the current bias against the dissolution of multiethnic states, the grievances of ethnic groups will have to be accommodated *within* the political institutions of existing countries. Moreover, given increasing codification of international norms on democratic forms of government as a fundamental human right, subnational group demands should be accommodated within a *democratic* form of government.[5]

Despite the conventional wisdom that democracy is difficult, if not impossible, in societies with deep ethnic enmities, consistent application of the modern principles of self-determination and democracy requires new thinking about ways to better harmonize these principles and new ways for the international community to encourage parties to adopt practical and appropriate practices to regulate ethnic conflicts. There is an urgent need to discover and refine practices that contain the inherent fissiparous tendencies that can tear multiethnic states apart, that foster tolerant and beneficial cultural diversity, and that (ideally) do so within a democratic framework. Even when mature democracy is not likely in a short time frame—as it is not, in a large proportion of existing states—the international community can exert pressure on nondemocratic states to adopt practices that can prevent the outbreak of violent ethnic conflict and move toward democratic forms of government. Failure to encourage harmony among groups will only generate new claims for self-determination.

Whereas some multiethnic societies have a relatively good track record of mediating their intergroup conflicts, others—referred to as deeply divided societies—have at times experienced bloody struggles and, in the worst instances, forced assimilation, "ethnic cleansing" or forced expulsion, and genocide. Some deeply divided societies wracked by violence for decades appear to be successfully moving toward more peaceful intergroup relations, as in South Africa, Northern Ireland, and possibly Bosnia-Herzegovina. Others are not, as the continuing ethnic violence in Sri Lanka, Sudan, Rwanda, and a host of other places demonstrates. Finally, many states, such as India, have experienced mixed or ambiguous success at ethnic conflict management but have maintained a democratic system in spite of severe intergroup differences and very difficult socioeconomic circumstances. Certainly not all ethnic conflicts involve claims to territorial self-determination, but those left inappropriately managed often degenerate to this extreme.

The task of ethnic conflict management is to create terms of intergroup coexistence that are consensual rather than coercive

(Esman 1994:2). Successful regulation of conflict in a multiethnic society occurs when the predominant pattern of intergroup dispute resolution is based on bargaining and reciprocity; unsuccessful regulation is evident when conflict degenerates into violence. A central challenge of managing ethnic conflict in the current era is to promote practices that successfully regulate competing group claims within a democratic framework—that is, those that allow for on-going, nonviolent bargaining by peoples who share a common state that offers regular, free, and fair elections, accountability and transparency, and security and human rights for its citizens.

In what ways can systems of democratic government be structured to ameliorate the destructive potential of ethnic conflicts? In what ways can group self-determination be meaningfully practiced without the creation of new sovereign states? How compatible are successful conflict-regulating practices in multiethnic societies with democratic norms of mass participation and competitive elections? How can the international community better promote management of ethnic conflicts and democratization simultaneously, without working at cross-purposes?

Many policymakers and scholars alike believe that broadly inclusive government, or power sharing, is essential to successful conflict management in societies beset by severe ethnic conflicts. Broadly interpreted, *power-sharing political systems are those that foster governing coalitions inclusive of most, if not all, major mobilized ethnic groups in society.* In severely divided societies, the chances of achieving representation of *all* political factions is inherently limited; even when some representatives of all major groups are included in governing coalitions, invariably there are other contending political leaders who claim to represent the group and refuse to share power with their ethnic adversaries. Thus, power-sharing political systems, particularly in the most deeply divided societies, are inclusive of *generally legitimate representatives of all groups.* Decision making is based on a consensus that transcends groups through coalitions that are widely inclusive. Consensus or near-consensus decision making is differentiated from majoritarian forms of democracy, in which decisions are taken for the entire society on the basis of the preferences of a minimum winning majority (Rae 1969).

The term *power sharing* has been defined by scholars such as Arend Lijphart as a set of principles that, when carried out through practices and institutions, provide every significant identity group or segment in a society representation and decision-making abilities on common issues and a degree of autonomy over issues of importance to the group. Lijphart's principles of power sharing—known as "consociational democracy" (derived from the Latin term *consociatio*, to associate in an alliance)—is pathbreaking in its differentiation of coalescent democracy from majoritarian democracy (Lijphart 1977a:25).

Scholars differ over whether the *consociational* power-sharing approach—in which groups are represented as groups (usually through ethnically exclusive political parties), in essence as building blocks of a common society—leads to better conflict management than the *integrative* (or pluralist) approach, in which practices seek to foster political organizations that transcend ethnic group differences. The integrative approach sees as ideal the creation of pre-election coalitions between ethnic parties or (less common) the creation of broad multiethnic parties on the basis of interests that transcend ethnic identities, such as region or common economic interests. Traditionally, pluralism also relies on the forces of economic interaction to help create social cleavages that crosscut ascriptive identity. The preeminent example is the crosscutting pattern of democracy in the multiethnic United States, best described in Seymour Martin Lipset's 1960 book *Political Man*.

In addition, preeminent scholars of the politics of multiethnic societies differ on the scope of the term *power sharing*. Some, such as Lijphart, argue that the consociational approach to power sharing encompasses a wide variety of practices and instances. Others, such as Donald Horowitz, argue that the consociational approach is more narrow in meaning and that many cases of consociational democracy cited by consociationalists (such as Malaysia or Lebanon) are in fact not consociational but integrative. Lijphart contends that the integrative approach is essentially majoritarian and that integrative mechanisms encourage majority representatives to behave moderately and with sensitivity toward minorities, which are still excluded from real political power.

Thus, the power-sharing debate revolves around the following central question: Which broad approach best manages conflict—one that essentially sees ethnic groups as building blocks of national politics in multiethnic states, or one that purposefully encourages the formation of political blocs across group lines? Consociationalists suggest that conflict management is best promoted by accommodation among ethnic group leaders representative of their communities through cooperative problem solving in postelection coalitions. Critics of the consociational approach—such as Horowitz (1985)—argue that the likelihood of violent conflict is reduced more effectively by institutions and practices that create incentives for the formation of preelection coalitions and that encourage intragroup competition rather than intergroup competition. Ideally, integrative mechanisms would lead to multiethnic parties or organizations that transcend narrow communal interests.

A central theme of this book is that the concept of power sharing encompasses both consociational power sharing *and* integrative power sharing, a point that is more fully developed in chapters 3 and 4. Both the consociational and the integrative approaches to ethnic conflict management seek to promote governing coalitions that are broadly *inclusive* of all ethnic groups in a deeply divided multiethnic society—the hallmark of power sharing—but advocates of these approaches sharply disagree over when and how such coalitions are formed and which specific institutions and practices better manage ethnic conflict. For this reason, power sharing should be interpreted as encompassing both approaches; the different types of institutions and practices for promoting democratic ethnic conflict management can be assembled and arranged in many different ways.

For policymakers, the debate among political scientists over approaches to power sharing, and indeed the very scope of the concept itself, may seem rather academic—filled with terminological exegeses, and irrelevant to the hard day-to-day decisions that must be made in dealing with contemporary ethnic conflicts. On the contrary, the power-sharing debate is critical to policy making. The fundamental policy principles and specific policy recommendations that emanate from these two basic approaches to successful ethnic conflict management in a democratic framework—such as the type of electoral system that parties to a conflict should be encouraged to adopt—are starkly different. Understanding the differences and formulating appropriate policies may spell the difference—for disputants and international intervenors alike—between successful ethnic conflict management and costly violent confrontation.

Successful interventions in ethnic conflicts, such as in Namibia, have been premised on a much better understanding of the underlying ethnic dynamics of a given situation than unsuccessful ones, such as in Somalia. In the former case, a clear set of constitutional principles for the conflict's outcome resulted in a political arrangement on which all parties could eventually agree. In Somalia, the United Nations had no clear vision of what kind of post-intervention Somali state should be created, and so the various factions were permitted to wallow in their differences. Surely one of the many elements of successful international intervention is having a clear sense of an appropriate outcome.

When faced with the vexing problems of ameliorating ethnic conflicts in multiethnic societies within a shared political framework, policymakers should focus on the following questions: What approach to power sharing (consociational or integrative) offers the better hope for ameliorating a given ethnic conflict, and which specific practices should be adopted? What are the pitfalls of power-sharing practices, and under what conditions does power sharing succeed or fail? Is power sharing based on elite accommodation inherently undemocratic? Under what circumstances should the international community urge or even coerce parties to ethnic conflicts to share power? If they do so, then how and at what point in the stages of escalation and de-escalation of ethnic conflict should power-sharing practices be encouraged?

This book does not endorse a simple model or set of detailed prescriptions to guide policymakers as they address the questions posed above. Instead, the book provides a general summary of the contemporary scholarly debate over power-sharing approaches and mechanisms and examines some recent (post–World War II) experiences with power sharing. The book offers a typology of democratic conflict-regulating practices that serves as a menu of options from which policymakers might choose as they confront the complexities of any given ethnic conflict. Finally, the book addresses a number of issues that arise when would-be conciliators of ethnic conflicts are confronted with the vexing problems of international intervention to encourage ethnic enemies to resolve their differences within a shared state and a minimally democratic framework.

Although much of this book is a summary and reconfiguration of recent scholarship on ethnic conflict and power sharing, the intent is to cogently present the analysis for consumption by policymakers and to contribute to the existing literature by addressing a heretofore unaddressed question: Under what conditions, and in what manner, should the international community promote power sharing as a means to prevent, manage, or resolve violent ethnic conflict? With this objective in mind, Alexander George has argued that generic knowledge and comparative empirical analysis can inform decision making, but it cannot substitute for detailed knowledge and practical experience with any given situation (1993a:19–29). This dictum certainly applies to the question of when the promotion of power sharing may or may not be an appropriate response to ethnic conflicts.

In an era in which ethnic conflict poses *the* central challenge to international peace, the significance of the power-sharing concept is clear: if ethnic groups can fulfill aspirations for self-determination *within* the boundaries of existing states by embracing appropriate democratic conflict-regulating practices, violent conflicts to create ever-more, ever-smaller homogeneous ethnic states can be forestalled. Even when democracy is unlikely, some of the practices identified in this book can be encouraged. In short, the principle of self-determination need not be such a vexing issue in international law and practice. As Ralph Steinhart suggests, when ethnic groups can exercise real influence in the affairs of multiethnic states, "the right of self-determination will be deemed protected *pro tanto.*

[Conversely,] the systematic exclusion of identity groups from the state would constitute a violation of the norm" (1994:30).

Power sharing, if defined broadly to encompass a wide range of practices that promote meaningful inclusivity and balanced influence for all major groups in a multiethnic society, is a potential answer to ethnic conflict management in many contemporary situations—such as in South Africa's current five-year interim government of national unity. But power-sharing practices are likely to have conflict-mitigating effects only if the disputants arrive at them through a process of negotiation and reciprocity that all significant parties perceive as fair and just, given their own changing interests and needs.

Equally, there are pitfalls in power-sharing agreements that may be premature, based on unrealistic expectations, agreed to with ill intent, or simply built on too narrow a foundation. The failed power-sharing pact in Rwanda (the 1993 Arusha Accord), brokered by the international community but never fully implemented before the country degenerated into genocidal ethnic strife, is a stark reminder of the limits of such agreements when ethnic relations are highly volatile and enmities simply run too deep.

2

Ethnic Conflict
Approaches, Patterns, and Dynamics

Scholarship and journalistic reporting on ethnic conflict have bal-
looned since the end of the Cold War, reflecting the experiences of
the era and the new challenges that ethnic struggles have created for
the international community.[1] Some of the old concepts used to
explain conflict in the international system during the Cold War,
such as the "security dilemma," are still useful. Barry Posen, in out-
lining the security dilemma faced by ethnic groups under conditions
of rapid change in the overarching rules of the game (that is, the
international system), penetratingly describes why ethnic groups
would turn to violence to counter real or perceived threats to group
security (1993).

Why do ethnic groups mobilize for political aims? Why are ethnic conflicts so severe and seemingly intractable? What are the patterns of ethnic conflict escalation and de-escalation, and in what
ways are they manifested? Are ethnic conflicts amenable to management, and if so, what principles apply? Although these questions—
the central concerns of scholars of ethnic conflict—cannot be fully
addressed here, a review of debate on these subjects will place the
analysis of power sharing in a larger context. Assumptions or beliefs
about the sources and manifestations of ethnic conflict have important ramifications for assessing whether power-sharing approaches
can help ameliorate group fears or temper chauvinism and, if so,
which approach and practices may work in different situations.

Approaches to Ethnic Conflict Analysis

Broadly construed, there are two schools of thought to explain the phenomenon of ethnic conflict. The first, termed *primordialism*, explains ethnicity in terms of inherited group behavioral characteristics that some scholars would argue are biologically based; that is, ethnic group identity is passed from generation to generation (van den Berghe 1981).[2] Others, known as *instrumentalists*, argue that ethnicity is contextual, fluid, and a function of structural conditions in society. Instrumentalists assert that ethnic identities wax and wane, contingent on a wide variety of variables, including the capacity and skills of political entrepreneurs who can effectively mobilize groups for collective aims and articulate beliefs about common ancestry and destiny. Some instrumentalists (alternatively known as structuralists) suggest that ethnic identity is socially constructed, often created or de-emphasized by power-seeking political elites in historically determined economic and social arrangements.[3] To the extent that ethnic identities are perceived as a given by these scholars, they are highly fluid, manipulable, and contextually dependent.

Instrumentalists often view ethnic conflict as less a matter of incompatible identities and more a consequence of (a) differential rates and patterns of modernization between groups and (b) competition over economic and environmental resources in situations where relations among groups vary according to wealth and social status. In other words, ethnicity is often a guise for the pursuit of essentially economic interests.

Using a psychocultural approach, Donald Horowitz, in his pioneering book *Ethnic Groups in Conflict*, stresses the importance of "relative group worth" in explaining ethnic group mobilization. This argument asserts that differences in perceptions of status are important in understanding the presence or absence of tensions between groups, especially when a given group's status is rapidly rising or falling. Horowitz, for example, distinguishes between "advanced" and "backward" groups on the basis of their technological and organizational capacities (1985:166) and draws attention to the differences between ranked and unranked systems of ethnic relations.

In debate about the nature of ethnicity, two important facts should be kept in mind. First, each identifiable ethnic conflict occurs in its own context as a result of unique historical developments, structural conditions (especially the structure of intergroup economic relations), and regional and international contexts. Generalizing across all cases with an all-encompassing theory is hazardous, as Stavenhagen (1994:15) rightly suggests. The extent to which scholars see ethnicity as immutable and innate versus socially constructed influences beliefs about the type of political systems that can best ameliorate conflict along ethnic lines. For example, the more rigid and intransigent the ethnic identities, the less likely that intergroup relations can be manipulated; a consociational approach may work best. On the other hand, if ethnic relations are volatile and rapidly changing, they may be amenable to integrative mechanisms. Volatile and rapidly changing ethnic relationships may spell trouble, as in the former Yugoslavia, or may present opportunities for conflict management, as in South Africa.

Analysts of ethnic conflict increasingly agree that the primordialist and instrumentalist approaches to ethnic identities are not mutually exclusive and can in fact be describing different sides of the same coin. Of course, within these broad categories there is a variety of nuanced differences; at best, one should consider the two poles of the debate about the nature of ethnic conflict—primordialism and instrumentalism—in terms of a spectrum. Thinking of ethnic conflict in this way can also help reconcile the oft-heard scholarly criticism that popular journalism is simplistic, sometimes referring to ancient animosities or historical hatreds as frozen during the Cold War and re-emerging in the current era once the totalitarian lid was removed. In sum, ethnicity is multifaceted and fluid; not only may any single individual possess more than one identity characteristic, but the boundaries of group identity can change dramatically over time.

What is most important is not whether ethnic group identity is innate and fixed or contrived and manipulable, it is that members of an ethnic group *perceive* the ethnic group to be real (Esman 1994; Stavenhagen 1994). Perceptions are critical in understanding the extent to which intergroup relations can be peaceful or violent.

Donald Rothchild rightly focuses on ethnic groups' perceptions of one another, identifying three basic types: an *essentialist* perception, in which groups perceive physical, cultural, or social threats to their vital interests—thereby making compromise seem a sign of weakness; *pragmatic* perceptions, in which conflicts of interest remain acute but compromise is possible on the margins; and *reciprocative* perceptions, in which groups "seek to transform the structure of relations to achieve mutual interest, primarily through the state as a mediator" (1986:87–93). Essentialist perceptions will likely lead to violent intergroup conflict, pragmatic perceptions allow for an occasional truce or cooperation in limited spheres, and reciprocative perceptions lay the foundation for long-term peaceful cooperation among groups. The important issue of changing perceptions in transitional moments is revisited in chapter 5.

Patterns of Ethnic Politics

Despite the wide range of scholarly approaches to describing the nature of ethnicity, it is possible to discern common patterns of ethnic politics that will help clarify the distinction between successfully regulated multiethnic societies and the violent intercourse of deeply divided societies. A clearer sense of the basic patterns of ethnic conflict may lead to more consistent policy prescriptions about what types of practices can help alleviate or manage tensions. In the analysis of any given situation of ethnic conflict, three issues arise: the structure of social "cleavages,"[4] the relationships between ethnic groups and the state, and the stages or phases of conflict escalation and de-escalation.

The *salience* of ethnicity as a social differentiator and the *intensity* of ethnic ties are critical predictors of violence. Salience and intensity are tied closely to the perceived stakes of ethnic relations (Esman 1994). What are the expected costs of defeat? What threats to group survival or well-being are perceived? Stakes are arguably highest when group identity is threatened or challenged—especially symbols of ethnic identity and destiny that are held as sacred to the group and are neither divisible nor amenable to compromise or trade-off. For this reason Horowitz refers to ethnic group claims on issues such as language as "incommensurate goods" not easily amenable to split-the-difference compromises (1985:219–224).

There is broad scholarly consensus that when social cleavages are reinforcing rather than overlapping, the potential for conflict is more acute. This is particularly so when the segments of a society are hierarchically arranged, that is, when one distinct group (or coalition of groups) dominates others (Huntington 1981). There is also good reason to believe that "dual societies," such as Rwanda or Sri Lanka, in which two ethnic groups compete for power in a zero-sum game, are especially intractable. The classic case of such a stratified, dual society, however, is apartheid South Africa, in which the structure of social cleavages was strongly reinforcing along lines of race and class but which has nonetheless proven tractable over the long term. Northern Ireland, too, is such a dual society, although the prospects for peace are better today than in the past twenty-five years.

The hallmark of a deeply divided society likely to experience significant and violent conflict is the presence of separate organizations that permeate and divide every aspect of society on the basis of identity. Horowitz points out that in divided societies "ethnic affiliations are powerful, permeative, passionate, and pervasive" (1985:12). Although virtually all societies contain a mix of voluntary associations (for example, trade unions) and ascriptive organizations (for example, religious institutions), a critical characteristic of civil society in deeply divided societies is the dearth of associations that transcend ethnic identities (Smith 1965; Rabushka and Shepsle 1972:21).[5]

Rabushka and Shepsle, in their pioneering work *Politics in Plural Societies: A Theory of Democratic Instability* (1972), offer a simple and useful typology of multiethnic societies based on the structure of ethnic cleavages and power relationships.[6] Following their analysis, I differentiate among four types of deeply divided societies as follows:

- *Fragmented.* In a fragmented society there are more than four major mobilized ethnic groups, none of which is clearly dominant. Examples of fragmented societies are Afghanistan, India, Nigeria, and Zaire.

- *Balanced.* Balanced societies, with four or fewer clearly identifiable groups, can be either bipolar (for example, Cyprus and Northern Ireland) or multipolar (for example, Bosnia).
- *Dominant minority.* A dominant minority can wield power to the exclusion of a significant majority. Examples include Rwanda, Burundi, Iraq, Syria, and white settler societies such as Rhodesia and South Africa. In some Latin American states, such as Guatemala, Haiti, and Peru, a Caucasian or mestizo minority has dominated indigenous majorities (although scholars differ over whether these are ethnic conflicts).
- *Dominant majority.* Societies in which a majority group dominates ethnic minorities are numerous, for example, in Croatia, Russia, Estonia, Sri Lanka, and Israel.

Although deep cleavages among ethnic groups often result in severe ethnic conflict, there is increasing recognition that one important variable in determining whether ethnic relations are based on pragmatism and reciprocity—that is, peacefully managed—is the nature of *within*-group differences. Some suggest that cohesive and confident ethnic groups—with clearly legitimate and broadly supported leadership—can deliver at the bargaining table, fostering moderation across ethnic lines. Others suggest that strong splits within an ethnic community ultimately facilitate conflict management because moderates within the group will form multiethnic coalitions with moderates of other groups, resulting in a broad and tolerant multiethnic core.

For both of these points of view, however, a key question is whether essentialist hard-liners or pragmatic accommodationists are ascendant in a given community and whether it is possible for moderates to emerge and form coalitions that can survive assaults by hard-liners. Those who believe in the efficacy of political engineering, such as Horowitz, suggest that the structure of the institutions can influence whether moderates or hard-liners will emerge ascendant.[7]

A common thread that runs through most analysis of ethnic conflict is the presence and role of ethnic entrepreneurs, political leaders who articulate beliefs in kinship bonds and common destiny and who mobilize and organize groups to press group claims. Ethnic entrepreneurs may be perceived as benign interest aggregators that serve a critical representative function, or as manipulative and exploitative power seekers that mobilize on ethnic themes for their own individual aggrandizement. In deeply divisive ethnic group relations, the problem of ethnic outbidding is pervasive. Extremist leaders, seeking to capitalize on mass resentment, outbid moderates by decrying acts of accommodation as a sellout of group interests, citing collective betrayal and humiliation.

The phenomenon of outbidding—and mass responsiveness to playing the ethnic card—is an especially acute problem for constructing intergroup relations in divided societies, precisely because a moderate multiethnic center is often unable to sustain itself against the centrifugal forces unleashed by the heated rhetoric of ethnic chauvinism.[8] A 1995 Human Rights Watch report argues that "time after time, [a] proximate cause of violence is governmental exploitation of communal differences. . . . The 'communal card' is frequently played, for example, when a government is losing popularity or legitimacy, and finds it convenient to wrap itself in the cloak of ethnic, racial, or religious rhetoric" (Human Rights Watch 1995:viii). Radical outbidding, whether by incumbent politicians or challengers, is found in every major ethnic conflict and is often the mainspring of discrimination and violence. When extreme chauvinist rhetoric resonates with popular attitudes, it leads to the "bankruptcy of moderation" (Rabushka and Shepsle 1972:86).

In addition to intragroup struggles over the soul of the nation, ethnic conflict is often a competition among groups for ownership of the state.[9] To what extent and in what manner does the state stand above and mediate ethnic conflict? Does an ethnically exclusive organization—a party, movement, or military force—control the state and wield power in the exclusive interest of the group? Does the state belong to a single ethnic group, or coalition of groups, to the exclusion (and usually the detriment) of out-groups?[10]

The relationship between the ethnic group and the state is a critical predictor of severe ethnic conflicts. Paul Brass writes, "Every state . . . tends to support particular groups, to distribute privileges unequally, and to differentiate among various categories in the population. . . . The state itself is the greatest prize and resource over which groups engage in a continuing struggle in societies that have not developed stable relationships among the main institutions and centrally organized social forces" (1985:9, 29). The expropriation of the symbols, power, and resources of the state to the exclusion of significant components of the population in multiethnic societies is a strong indicator of the likelihood of ethnic violence: group membership for some is an entitlement system of state-sanctioned status and wealth. Patterned inequality and discrimination, usually reinforced by public policy, is argued by some analysts to be the greatest predictor of violence in ethnic conflicts (Gurr 1993). Once ethnic parties seize control of the state, they often manipulate the allocation of resources to the exclusive advantage of their group, further exacerbating tensions (Esman 1986).

For these reasons, ethnic group grievances are commonly targeted at the state, either for minor changes in the rules of interaction—for example, more equitable resource distribution—or for more drastic change, such as political divorce through boundary change. Esman correctly asserts that "the territorial state has everywhere become the arena in which competing ethnic groups' claims are asserted, contested, and regulated. . . . Rules established and enforced by the state determine the goals that ethnic communities may legitimately pursue and the strategies and tactics they may employ. . . . The state, then, is a party to most contemporary ethnic conflicts" (1994:18, 19).

The territorial dimension of ethnic conflict is a central theme in the scholarly literature.[11] Conflicts in which groups claim exclusive title of territory for control or access are generally perceived to be more intractable than those in which there is a high degree of interdependence and integration. For ethnic groups, conflict over territory is usually zero sum, especially when territory is associated with symbolic or psychocultural aspects of group solidarity. Perhaps the preeminent example of seemingly irreconcilable claims to territory in the modern world is Jerusalem, where competing claims are based on deeply rooted beliefs and ancient religious claims. For many groups simultaneously, the territory is sacred and must be possessed.

Although competing territorial claims are conceivably negotiable and land can be apportioned and reapportioned, even (potentially) in Jerusalem, the ideological and religious dimensions of such claims are usually not amenable to simple split-the-difference compromises. For this reason, conflicts with a strong territorial dimension are more likely to lead to the vexing problems of secession, irredentism, and ethnic cleansing or forced expulsion.

Increasingly, analysts of ethnic conflicts are focusing on the transnational linkages of intergroup relations. Indeed, there is a burgeoning literature on the internationalization of ethnic conflict and the transnational linkages through which many ethnic groups derive critical moral and material support.[12] Ethnic conflicts are internationalized as a result of cross-border kinship ties, diaspora politics, humanitarian concerns, environmental fallout from violent conflict, and economic disruption. In many instances—such as Afghanistan, Kashmir, Sri Lanka, the former Yugoslavia, the former Soviet Union,[13] Rwanda, and Burundi, just to name a few—ethnic conflicts are fueled and complicated by strong bonds that link groups across borders. For example, the conflict between Tamil separatists and the government of Sri Lanka is increasingly spilling over into the nearby Indian state of Tamil Nadu, causing intensified internal problems of cohesion in India and seriously complicating attempts to resolve the civil war peacefully in Sri Lanka. Separatist rebels allegedly have free rein in parts of Tamil Nadu to prepare and launch attacks in Sri Lanka.

Globalization has resulted in ever-increasing diaspora communities in both Western and developing societies; they are sometimes treated in a responsive manner by the host state and responsibly integrated or assimilated into society, but in other instances they are not. When diasporas are close in proximity, as in host-kin situations—such as Hungarians who live in neighboring Slovakia or Romania—internal ethnic disputes become quickly internationalized, drawing in neighboring states, regional organizations, and the international community. As the very terms *host* and *kin* imply, full and equal citizenship for ethnic minorities is often a severely contentious issue.

When citizenship is defined in ethnic terms in a multiethnic society, myriad problems arise. That is, who "belongs" in a given state is as important a question as who happens to live there; when the two do not coincide, the propensity for conflict is especially high. Citizenship issues centered on ethnicity and tensions between neighbors are an important problem throughout Eastern Europe. Herbert Okun points out that "a key aspect of the [ethnic conflict] situation in Macedonia is neighboring Albania's attitudes and actions regarding its ethnic kinfolk inside Macedonia."[14] In chapter 6, I suggest that these linkages may complicate ethnic conflict management, but they may also be avenues for international action to promote ethnic accommodation.

The transnational dimensions of ethnic conflict are important in other respects. The modern state is not a closed system, impervious to effects from beyond its borders. For that reason, ethnic conflict is increasingly of special concern to the international community beyond humanitarian impulses to prevent or treat the maladies of violent conflict. Growing regional economic and political integration, the globalization of the international economy, and modern communications have eroded traditional notions of state sovereignty and the doctrine of noninterference enshrined in the UN Charter. However, even as regional integration and globalism may influence the nature of intergroup relations within states, the modern state is not about to wither away. Although governments do not fully control economic policy and may exercise limited control in spheres such as communication and transnational linkages, they continue, as Esman writes, "to remain arenas, targets, and usually parties to ethnic-based conflicts" (1994:217).

Escalation and De-escalation

At what stage of escalation or de-escalation is an ethnic conflict? The experience of the post–Cold War world—especially the conflict in the former Yugoslavia—clearly shows that times of transition (both in the international system and in states) can be perilous for ethnic relations; they can deteriorate into intractable warfare at an unexpectedly precipitous rate. Previously accommodative ethnic group relations (measured by indicators such as high rates of inter-ethnic marriages—for example, among Bosnians prior to the civil war) can quickly become very intolerant and very violent. More-over, the experience of Somalia suggests that even in states that are considered comparatively homogeneous, identity conflicts—in this case along subethnic, or clan, cleavages—can emerge that plunge society into anarchy and precipitate the "failure" of states (Helman and Ratner 1992–1993; Rothchild 1995).

But, contrary to the conventional wisdom, the post–Cold War era equally demonstrates the opposite point: that long-standing eth-nic conflicts can de-escalate and that relations among ethnic groups can improve and become more accommodative and less violent. The transformation of South Africa from a quintessential deeply divided society under apartheid to a model of intergroup accommo-dation in five short years is dramatic. Moves toward rapprochement in the Northern Ireland and Israel-Palestine conflicts reinforce this conclusion. Clearly, these conflicts were intractable for many, many years, and their improvement is only a fairly recent event. Never-theless, dire predictions of a steady slide into anarchy in third world states are not borne out by the wide range of cases in which ethnic conflicts have escalated, de-escalated, or remained stagnant in recent years.

This diversity of direction in the dynamics of ethnic conflict leads scholars and analysts to address the questions Under what circum-stances do ethnic conflicts escalate into violence? and Under what circumstances do they become amenable to peaceful management through pragmatic negotiation and, ideally, reciprocity?

Given recent experience with escalating ethnic conflicts, scholars and analysts are developing better ways of identifying common pat-terns of escalation in ethnic conflicts. A critical distinction is between the *background conditions* of an ethnic conflict, that is, the range of variables described above, and *escalatory dynamics* (Väyrynen and Leatherman 1995:10), the progression of moves and countermoves that lead groups away from cooperation and toward violence. Within the scope of background conditions are the seven early warning indicators of acute ethnic conflict identified by Väyrynen and Leatherman (1995:60–61): (1) the degree of structural tension in society; (2) whether territory is shared or divided; (3) nature of social cleavages, overlapping or crosscutting; (4) legitimacy of political governance; (5) cultural tension; (6) level of governmental repression and countermobilization along group lines; and (7) the influence of external actors.[15] In addition, they identify *vertical escalation* as an increase in the magnitude or intensity of a dispute (usually measured in terms of deaths or injuries in political violence) and *horizontal escalation*, which is a broadening of the conflict to new groups, states, or communities.

When the background conditions for ethnic conflict exist, events—known as triggers—may cause intergroup relations to move from pragmatic to essential, from relative accommodation to hostility and violence. Conflict triggers can include provocative acts by political leaders, failed elections, abrupt changes in the regional security environment, or violent upsurges such as riots. Northup (1989) describes the sequential moves that lead parties to deepen or broaden their conflicts, such as perceptions of threat and distortion of intention, followed by rigidification of identity perceptions and expectations that opposing groups will inflict harm unless offensive or defensive action is taken.[16] Richard Goldstone, the international special prosecutor who is investigating genocide in the former Yugoslavia and in Rwanda and who conducted inquiries into political violence in his native South Africa, finds that patterns of social discrimination set the stage for ethnic violence, allowing normally peaceful and tolerant people to forgo social norms against violence and lash out against their ethnic enemies.

When ethnic groups do mobilize for offensive or defensive purposes, a countermobilization by opponents usually follows. For this reason, Esman describes escalation of ethnic conflicts as a recursive phenomenon. He writes: "Ethnic mobilization may set in motion collective behavior that cannot be manipulated by the mobilizers, but triggers violence that exacerbates inter-ethnic hostility or antagonisms between an ethnic movement and the state" (1994:31). In many ethnic conflicts, violence is a recurring or cyclical problem. Burundi is currently undergoing its sixth major convulsion of violence since independence in 1962, demonstrating how strife can be self-reinforcing, escalating in a spiral in which each upsurge of intergroup violence sets the stage for the next round of killing. Even after a presumably stable and acceptable peace has been attained, as in Sudan in 1972, ethnic conflicts can recur if one party unilaterally alters the terms of a peace agreement for short-term gains.

Escalation of ethnic conflicts is perhaps more easily understood than de-escalation. Whether a party to a conflict achieves a victory or is defeated, or whether parties fight to exhaustion and stalemate, ethnic conflicts can gradually contract and become less violent. Principal among the causes of conflict de-escalation is the willingness of conflicting parties to avoid mutually damaging violence. Thomas Schelling (1960:5) writes: "If war to the finish has become inevitable, there is nothing left but pure conflict; but if there is any possibility of avoiding a mutually damaging war, of conducting warfare in a way that minimizes damage, or of coercing an adversary by threatening war rather than waging it, the possibility of a mutual accommodation is as important and dramatic as the element of conflict." In deeply divided societies, the realization that further escalation of a conflict will result in mutually damaging outcomes has been referred to by Lijphart as the "self-negating prophecy." He writes that "elites co-operate in spite of the segmental differences dividing them because to do otherwise would mean to call forth the prophesied consequences of the plural character of the society" (1977a:100).

Barring complete victory or defeat—which in ethnic conflict implies genocidal obliteration of the opponent, subjugation, involuntary expulsion, or forced assimilation—de-escalation of a conflict evolves in a series of phases or stages of bargaining or negotiation, which can be overlapping and mutually reinforcing (Kriesberg 1989; Zartman 1991).[17] International conflict management specialists describe de-escalation processes in "protracted social conflicts," in which an identity group cannot be definitively defeated (Azar and Burton 1986), in terms of the following phases or stages:

- The escalation of strife into a *mutually hurting stalemate*. Given the structural condition of a stalemate, and given a series of precipitating events that lead a conflict to a condition of ripeness for resolution (such as a conciliatory gesture by a moderate political leader), parties may begin to view an end to violent conflict in mutually beneficial terms.

- The subsequent stage of de-escalation is prenegotiation, or "talks about talks" (Stein 1989). In this phase, parties explore the range of potentially positive-sum outcomes and discuss preconditions to formal or direct negotiation.

- A successful prenegotiation stage can lead to the onset of *formal* or *direct negotiation*, in which parties negotiate a new set of rules of interaction and seek to alternatively structure their patterns of interaction in more peaceful ways. Successful formal or direct negotiation may lead to interim settlements or agreements—mutual security pacts—or more definitive or comprehensive settlements that establish basic or constitutional arrangements.[18]

- An often-neglected phase of de-escalation is the *implementation* or *peace-building phase*, in which the terms of settlement are acted on and the new patterns of interaction are routinized. This phase is critical precisely because ethnic conflicts tend to recur and because negotiated settlements are arguably unsustainable in civil strife (Wagner 1993).

I will return to the preeminent role of process in conflict de-escalation in chapters 5 and 6 in the context of strategies for mediator intervention to promote conflict-regulating practices in deeply divided societies; two further points deserve to be highlighted and reinforced here. First, there are some common elements of politics in deeply divided societies: the presence of ethnic entrepreneurs who mobilize the masses using identity politics; radical outbidding and flanking of moderates; manipulation of identity; changing perceptions and group boundaries; complex relationships between ethnicity and class; linkages among groups across borders and even continents; and the preeminent role of the state as the arbiter of ethnic relations.

Second, given these elements, ethnic conflicts are often perceived as intractable when in fact they are potentially tractable, given the right mix of structural circumstances, political leadership, and willingness of leaders and followers to avoid costly violence. In the post–Cold War world there are myriad examples to buttress this conclusion: states have imploded or become severely crippled under the weight of ethnic conflict (for example, Rwanda, Somalia, Liberia, Bosnia, Georgia, Afghanistan, Tajikistan, Sudan, and Iraq); some have experienced mixed results from conflict management or have remained static, but conflict could easily escalate (for example, Cyprus and Macedonia); and some have experienced unambiguous movement toward more peaceful relations (for example, Eritrea and Ethiopia, Cambodia, Northern Ireland, Israel and Palestine, and South Africa).

3

Democracy and Its Alternatives in Deeply Divided Societies

More often than not, conflict has been managed in divided societies through authoritarian domination of a group or groups over others. The approach is usually an exclusive one, in which minority (or sometimes, majority) communities are not provided the opportunity to directly or indirectly influence decisions made for the society as a whole. The approach may be revolutionary, attempting to remove the minority or majority factor from political life through forced assimilation (as Bulgaria recently sought to do with its Turkish minority) or genocidal. Other strategies that fall in the hegemonic approach include subjugation, isolation, avoidance, and displacement of ethnic groups (Rothchild and Olurunsola 1986:240–41).[1] Countless tyrannies have resorted to such measures, either singularly or in combination. In Thailand, Burma, and the Philippines, military rule has at times served, as Horowitz (1993:27) argues, as a mask for ethnic dominance.

Although subjugation and dominance are more common in practice, and non-Western examples of the democratic management of conflict in divided societies are few, there are instances of relatively successful ethnic conflict management within autocratic systems. Milton Esman notes that "historically some polities have succeeded rather well in managing ethnic cleavages by methods that include power-sharing methods. The autocratic Ottoman Empire governed for half a millennium. Under the 'millet' system it guaranteed a large measure of autonomy (self-determination and self-management) to its non-Muslim communities."[2] In India under British Colonial rule, power-sharing practices such as communal electoral rolls and reserved legislative seats were instituted. Of particular interest is the 1916 Lucknow Pact between the Indian National Congress and the Muslim League, which established under the overall suzerainty of the British Raj a system of Hindu-Muslim power sharing that helped mitigate communal conflict for several years before it broke down under the weight of communal violence (Wolpert 1992:294–309).

In a different manner, in some postcolonial African regimes an informal balancing act by autocratic regimes resulted in roughly proportional allocation of power and resources to ethnic groups. Rothchild terms these "hegemonic exchange" regimes (1986, 1995).[3] According to Rothchild, many one-party or no-party African states in the postcolonial era, such as Tanzania, Zambia, Kenya, Ivory Coast, and Cameroon, belong to this category (1995:59).[4]

In short, in many multiethnic states democracy is absent, but governments perform an implicit or even explicit informal balancing act, careful to include members of key ethnic groups at high levels in central governments and to distribute resources in a balanced manner, but tightly controlling democratic freedoms. For example, Singapore and Indonesia have arguably managed to balance competing ethnic claims, but these are certainly not liberal democracies.

Within consensual, noncoercive approaches to ethnic conflict management there are but two broad options: partition or democracy. Partition, which is rare and even more rarely peaceful, is in Lijphart's terms a "solution of the last resort" (1985:34).[5] The breakup of the Czechoslovak federation in 1992 on reasonably amicable terms supports the view that partition is an option within the noncoercive framework, even though other examples of state breakup—such as Eritrea or the former Yugoslavia—usually result from hardwon military victories or precipitate protracted civil war among the conflicting parties (as in Sudan, Sri Lanka, or more recently in the Russian republic of Chechnya). Partition *is* a viable option in deeply divided societies when ethnic groups are homogeneously concentrated in territory, when the new states themselves do not include significant minorities themselves, and when the rump state is willing to allow the secession to occur—conditions that are rarely met. I return to the issue of separation versus sharing in chapter 6.

If peaceful partition is an unlikely and highly unusual outcome in divided societies, and authoritarian methods are (normative concerns aside) at best a short-term solution to the management of ethnic conflicts, multiethnic societies need democracy by default. Yet the conventional wisdom, articulated by democrats such as John Stuart Mill in 1861, is that a "united public opinion" is necessary for democracy, and for that reason democracy is ill suited to multiethnic societies ([1861] 1958:230). That is, most multiethnic societies lack the political culture—defined as prerequisite values—that engender democracy.[6] Esman writes:

> Critics of democracy assert that open competitive politics facilitate the politicization of ethnic communities and the consequent danger of interethnic extremism and violent destabilization of the political order. They maintain that authoritarian methods and a strong state are needed to restrain ethnic politics in divided and conflict-prone societies. This notion is a frequent justification for military rule and for one-party regimes in ethnically plural societies, including Tito's rule in Yugoslavia, the KANU [Kenyan African National Union] dictatorship in Kenya, and the Suharto-New Order government in Indonesia [1994:41].

When thoughtful analysts have looked at the challenges created by the patterns of politics in deeply divided societies, outlined above, it is no surprise that they have come to the conclusion rhetorically framed by Rabushka and Shepsle: "Is the resolution of intense but conflicting preferences in the [deeply divided] society manageable in a democratic framework? We think not" (1972:217).

No analyst argues that politics in deeply divided societies facilitates democracy or that conditions for it are favorable in the vast majority of today's multiethnic societies. What drives analysts to consider democratic practices in situations of deep ethnic conflict is the belief that there are no viable alternatives to democracy as a system of just and stable conflict management. Lijphart (1977a:277) writes: "Not only have non-democratic regimes failed to be good nation-builders;

they have not even established good records of maintaining order and peace in plural societies."

Where ethnic tensions have been successfully managed, the regime is open and respectful of human rights and features a participatory civil society, universal suffrage, free and fair elections, and a modicum of fairness in the distribution of economic resources. In addition, patterns of reciprocal interactions among competing ethnic groups are institutionalized through the widely accepted and consensually framed rules of the political game. Stated differently, when the state stands above ethnic conflicts and mediates them, employing democratic institutions and practices, differences among communities can be worked out in parliament rather than on the streets. The telltale sign of successful conflict management in multiethnic societies is widespread commitment to the mediation of disputes through the democratic rules of the game.[7]

Problems of Majoritarian Democracy

At least one hallmark of a democratic system is the willingness of the principal interests in society to accept the inherently uncertain consequences of the electoral game. The electoral arena in a democracy is the most important element of politics, because it is the primary forum of intergroup competition. It is in the halls of parliament, not in the streets, that individuals and groups in multiethnic societies are expected to arbitrate their differences. Robert Dahl describes the importance of *mutual security* as a prerequisite to electoral competition and the need for minimum level of the protection of basic interests (or rights) so that defeat at the ballot box will not jeopardize physical survival (1973).

Clearly, the Algerian military leadership perceived a threat to its power, and potentially to physical survival, when in January 1992 it stepped in to cancel the second round of balloting that would in all probability have led to an absolute parliamentary majority for the Islamist Front for Islamic Salvation (FIS). Although the principal difference in Algeria is not between ethnic groups but between opinions on the desirability of an Islamic state, this case highlights the principal problem with democracy in instances where social divisions on ethnic or religious lines run deep. Absent Dahl's prerequisite of mutual security, elections are perceived by groups in conflict as a zero-sum game; it is a winner-take-all contest. Often, an election is perceived as an opportune moment for politicians to manipulate ethnicity in order to retain power, as in Kenya and Ghana in recent years.

In many divided societies, electoral competition is a contest for ownership of the state. Minorities, particularly, equate democracy not with freedom or participation but with the structured dominance of adversarial majority groups. Permanent minorities such as Tamils in Sri Lanka, Catholics in Northern Ireland, and whites in South Africa have feared the consequences of electoral competition, especially when the expected consequence of majority victory is discrimination against them. For minority groups, losing an election is a matter of not simply losing office but of losing the means for protecting the survival of the group.

In other types of voting, governments do not countenance plebiscites or referenda on secessionist claims because they fear the consequences of determining the popular will by simple majority rule. The government of India has not allowed the implementation of the UN General Assembly resolutions of 1947 promising a plebiscite on the territorial dispensation of Kashmir because of the likelihood that a majority of Muslims would opt for accession to Pakistan or, more recently, independence. The primary trigger in the onset of the war in Bosnia was the move in February 1992 by the predominantly Muslim and Croat government to hold a referendum on independence from the former Yugoslavia, the outcome of which would have been determined by simple majority rule; the referendum was boycotted by the Bosnian Serbs. Moreover, as Herbert Okun notes, "the referendum was held in breach of the constitution of Bosnia and Hercegovina, which required that major decisions of this nature were to be decided on the basis of consensus among the three 'constituent peoples' (Bosnian Muslims, Bosnian Serbs, Bosnian Croats)."[8]

The problem is that ethnic groups in conflict all too often associate elections and referenda, and democracy in general, with the principle of simple majority rule. Majoritarian democracy is typified by the Westminster system of small single-member districts with first-past-the-post (plurality) electoral rules; the party (or parties, in coalition governments) with a majority of the seats forms the government while other parties remain in loyal opposition. Analytically, there are three problems with simple majoritarian democracy in divided societies: the possibility of permanent exclusion of minority group-based political parties, the lack of "floating" voters whose preferences are formed on other-than-ascriptive criteria such as class,[9] and the pervasiveness of radical outbidding on divisive ethnic issues. Although simple majority rule may be fairest from a theoretical point of view (Rae 1969), the scholarly consensus recognizes the principle's limitations in divided societies.[10] (Horowitz [1993:30] also demonstrates how a procedurally free and fair election can lead to equally exclusive minority rule.)

Advocates of power sharing in divided societies agree on the dangers of majoritarianism, citing the potential distortions in vote-to-seat outcomes, the inability of geographically dispersed minority parties to achieve representation, and—in the context of an ethnic party system—the likelihood that a single ethnic group or coalition of ethnic groups will govern exclusively and to the detriment of others.[11] Lijphart, the most indefatigable critic of majoritarian and plurality electoral rules for divided societies (and indeed for other democracies), identifies the core problem when he refers to the potential for "majority dictatorship" (1985:102). Horowitz concurs, aruging in his seminal work, *Ethnic Groups in Conflict*, that under conditions of simple majority rule, "Ethnic parties developed, majorities took power, and minorities took shelter. It was a fearful situation, in which the prospect of minority exclusion from government underpinned by ethnic voting, was potentially permanent. . . . Civil violence, military coups, and the advent of single party regimes can all be traced to this problem of inclusion-exclusion" (1985:629).

Simply put, simple majority rule results in minimum winning coalitions that tend to exclude a significant minority; when minority preferences are intense and there is little chance of the minority becoming a majority, a recipe for conflict exists. Simple majoritarianism in a deeply divided society leads to zero-sum politics (Welsh 1993). The Westminster system of government-and-opposition, transplanted into many societies that were once part of the British empire, assumes that the opposition will be loyal and that the opportunity for alternation in winning coalitions is real. Without an assurance that the electoral system will not lead to permanent exclusion, why *should* a minority group that perceives a threatening environment be willing to accept the inherent risks of electoral competition?

Rejection of majoritarian democracy does not mean a rejection of democratic values. What distinguishes advocates of majoritarianism from advocates of coalescent democracy, or power sharing, is belief in the prospects for "political engineering" (Sartori 1968) to mitigate conflicts in divided societies. That is, the rules of the political game can be structured to institutionalize moderation on divisive ethnic themes, to contain the destructive tendencies, and to preempt the centrifugal thrust created by ethnic politics. There is no assertion that deft political engineering can prevent or eradicate deep enmities, but appropriate institutions can nudge the political system in the direction of reduced conflict and greater governmental accountability. The common assumption is that choices over the basic rules of the game affect its outcomes. Horowitz writes, "Where there is some determination to play by the rules, the rules can restructure the system so the game itself changes" (1985:601). The essence of power sharing is not to do away with democratic competition but to contain it within acceptable boundaries so that differences of opinion along ethnic lines do not ineluctably lead to intergroup violence.

The central question of political engineering is this: In deeply divided societies, which kinds of institutions and practices create an incentive structure for ethnic groups to mediate their differences through the legitimate institutions of a common democratic state? Alternatively, how can the incentive system be structured to reward and reinforce political leaders who moderate on divisive ethnic themes and to persuade citizens to support moderation, bargaining, and reciprocity among ethnic groups?

As highlighted in chapter 1, there are two distinct approaches to constructing conflict-ameliorating democratic institutions in deeply divided societies: the consociational model most associated with Lijphart (1968, 1969, 1977a, 1977b, 1985) and what I term the integrative approach associated with Horowitz (1985, 1990a, 1990b, 1991, 1993). These approaches are summarized in table 1. Although dichotomizing these approaches may be a too-simplistic description of their advocates' views, I do so here to highlight the differences. The former approach places greater faith in assurances for minority group protection, whereas the latter places greater emphasis on the role of incentives in encouraging interethnic co-operation. What unites them is the belief in coalescent democracy as an alternative to the adverse effects of majoritarianism and the assumptions that support a rejection of majoritarian practices. "Coalescent" decision making is argued to be a better prescription for the ills that plague deeply divided societies than the adversarial pattern associated with majoritarian democracy.[12]

Power Sharing: The Consociational Approach

Consociationalism, above all, relies on *elite cooperation* as the principal characteristic of successful conflict management in deeply divided societies.[13] Consociationalists suggest that even if there are deep communal differences, overarching integrative elite cooperation is a necessary and sufficient condition to assuage conflict. Eric Nordlinger (1972:73) goes so far as to argue that elites "alone can initiate, work out and implement conflict-regulating practices, therefore they alone can make direct and positive contributions to conflict-regulating outcomes." In the consociational approach, elites, or conflict group leaders, directly represent various societal segments and act to forge political ties at the center. This is the case in many of the consociational democracies—Belgium, the Netherlands, Switzerland, Malaysia (1955–1969), Lebanon (1943–1975)—that these theorists have considered successful experiences.[14] Advocates of consociationalism find the notion of nation building, or integrative approaches, a dubious proposition, citing the salience and rigidity of ethnic identity. To create a sense of common destiny when there is none entails both the breakdown of group loyalties

Table 1. Approaches to Power Sharing

	Consociational	Integrative
Characteristics	Elites cooperate after elections to form multiethnic coalitions and manage conflict; groups are autonomous; minorities are protected.	Parties encouraged to create coalitions before elections, creating broadly inclusive but majoritarian governments.
Principles	Broad-based or "grand" coalitions, minority veto, proportionality in allocation of civil service positions and public funds, group autonomy.	Dispersion and devolution of power, promotion of intraethnic competition, inducements for interethnic cooperation, policies to encourage alternative social alignments, managed distribution of resources.
Institutions and practices to promote these principles and effects	Parliamentary government, proportional representation of seats, proportional representation electoral system.	Federalism, vote pooling, electoral systems, president elected by "supermajority."
Strengths of the approach	Provides groups firm guarantees for the protection of their interests.	Provides politicians with incentives for moderation—"coalitions of commitment."
Weaknesses	"Coalitions of convenience." Elites may pursue conflict rather than try to reduce it; communal groups may not defer to their leaders; system relies on constraints against immoderate politics.	Lack of whole-country empirical examples of working systems; assumption that politicians respond to incentives and citizens will vote for parties not based on their own group.

and the creation of new ones, a Herculean task unlikely to be achieved in most instances.

According to Lijphart, consociationalism relies on four basic principles: a broad-based or "grand" coalition executive; minority veto; proportionality in the allocation of civil service positions and public funds; and group autonomy. Lijphart argues persistently that the institutions that give life to these principles must be specially adapted to the society they are to serve, and they cannot be implemented and expected to work singularly. Lijphart also identifies a number of conditions that are favorable to the successful operation of consociational democracy: popular deference to elites, "a multiple balance of power, small size of the country involved, overarching loyalties, segmental isolation, prior traditions of elite accommodation, and—although much more weakly and ambiguously—the presence of cross-cutting cleavages" (1977a:54). Lijphart's four basic principles are fleshed out a bit here:

1. *Broad-based parliamentary coalitions.* Power sharing in the executive in a grand coalition, or a variant thereof, ensures that the minority is not permanently excluded from political power.[15] Parliamentary systems are argued to be more conducive to the creation of inclusive governing coalitions. In grand coalitions, political elites—representing the various segments of society—thrash out their differences in an effort to reach consensus, but *public* contestation among them is limited. The common denominator and the most important feature is that decision making takes place consensually at the top among elites representing underlying social segments (Lijphart 1977a:31–36).

2. *Minority or mutual veto.* The second feature of consociationalism is the mutual or minority veto, through which each segment is given "a guarantee that it will not be outvoted by the majority when its vital interests are at stake" (Lijphart 1977b:118). Through the mutual veto, the majority's ability to rule is qualified by "negative minority rule" (Lijphart 1977a:36). The minority veto is at the heart of the concrete assurances of consociationalism. The veto provides an ironclad guarantee of

political protection to each segment on issues related to its vital interests. While the minority veto gives minorities the right to prevent action by others on the most sensitive issues, such as language, cultural rights, or education rights, it also serves a more important overriding goal. Like the Calhounian "concurrent majority," it invests each segment with the power of protecting itself (Lijphart 1977a:37).

3. *Proportionality*. In every sphere of political life, the principle of proportionality lies behind consociational practices. Proportionality is introduced at every level of government decision making (central, regional, and local) to give minority groups power, participation, and influence commensurate with their overall size in society. The principle is manifested in two ways. First, through the electoral system, proportional representation is used to faithfully translate the demographic strength of the segments into commensurate representation in parliament; parties are awarded seats in parliament in direct proportion to votes garnered in an election. Second, the allocation of resources by the state—including the appointment of civil servants and public spending—should be doled out according to the pro-portionality principle.

4. *Segmental group autonomy*. Through either territorial federal-ism or "corporate federalism" (nonterritorial autonomy), consociationalism provides internal autonomy for all groups who want it by devolving decision-making authority to the segments. Lijphart draws distinctions between those issues that concern the common interest and those that primarily concern the segments. On the former, decisions are made by consensus; otherwise, decision-making power is delegated to the seg-ments. The basic principle underlying communal autonomy is "rule by the minority over itself in the area of the minority's exclusive concern" (Lijphart 1977a:41). An important feature of the call for entrenched group rights on certain issues is the principle of "voluntary affiliation." Group identification should not be predefined or determined; instead the segments

of society would be able to define themselves through the proportional electoral system (Lijphart 1995).

Lijphart consistently asserts that consociationalism is the *only*
viable option for democracy in divided societies: "For many plural
societies of the non-Western world, therefore, the realistic choice is
not between the British [majoritarian] model of democracy and the
consociational model, but between consociational democracy and
no democracy at all" (1977a:238). Consociationalism, of course, is
not without its critics. Later in this chapter and in chapter 4, I
address criticisms of some of the specific practices (versus principles)
that are raised in response to the policy recommendations that flow
from consociationalism, but here I raise three broad drawbacks of
the consociational *approach* in order to better highlight the differences
between it and the integrative approach. Those drawbacks are the
reliance on elite accommodation and the problem of elite-initiated
conflict; the reification of ethnic identity; and the tendency toward
antidemocratic and inefficient decision making. (A fourth broad
criticism raised by Horowitz—that consociationalism relies on constraints, not incentives—is outlined in the next section.)

Consociationalists have been criticized for the assertion that elites
can effectively regulate conflict in divided societies. As the Anglo-
Irish Agreement of 1985 demonstrates—as does the 1990 failure of
the Meech Lake Accord agreed to by Canada's provincial leaders in
1987—even though political elites may agree on a formula for
accommodation, peace cannot endure without grass roots backing.
In Northern Ireland the 1985 Anglo-Irish Agreement portending
power sharing was reached without the inclusion of local Ulster,
unionist, Protestant involvement; this constituency perceived the
agreement, negotiated by the United Kingdom on its behalf, as a
step toward a unified Ireland. As Rose (1990:148) has suggested,
"exclusion from the deliberations was regarded as part of a deliberate British plan to 'sell out' the Protestant majority." Moreover,
George Tsebelis (1990) suggests that consociational institutions
may provide incentives for politicians to foment what he terms
"elite-initiated conflict"—conflict along group lines in order to

bolster their own bargaining position vis-à-vis other groups at the political center.

In a similar vein, Steven Burg is critical of consociationalism as the "ultimate form of elite manipulation and control," reducing the accountability of political leaders to their communities. He writes:

> There is mounting evidence that consociational arrangements (power sharing and mutual veto) encourage elites to rule in opposition to mass beliefs. Why did Yugoslavia and Czechoslovakia fall apart? It was not because of . . . inter-ethnic hatreds at the mass level. It was because of elite mobilization of latent nationalisms, and because the structural characteristics of each system included power sharing and mutual veto, enabling [for example] the Slovene regional leadership and the Slovak regional leadership to paralyze their respective federal governments. Yugoslavia, in particular, was an extreme example of the kind of power sharing advocated by the consociationalists. Peaceful/common solutions to intergroup and interregional conflicts were precluded in the Yugoslav/Czechoslovak cases by the actions of determined secessionists, not by the presence of spontaneous hatreds at the mass level. . . . The mass electorates did not want their respective countries to break up until elites had pushed these conflicts beyond the point of no return.[16]

Critics also assert that consociationalism serves to maintain, legitimize, and strengthen segmental claims against the state, reinforcing and entrenching ethnicity in the political system. By freezing group boundaries in the political system—for example, through statutory reservation of offices for specific group representatives—a consociational power-sharing system is said to be an undynamic model for conflict management (Barry 1975). Providing structural guarantees for communities (for example, through a minority veto) can provide systemic incentives for maintaining the rigidity of the segments. The Lebanese National Pact of 1943 (see chapter 4) is often cited as a stark reminder of the need to keep power-sharing practices as flexible as possible. Finally, consociational institutions are arguably antidemocratic because they can stifle vigorous opposition politics. For example, the absence of an opposition party in a grand coalition may detract from the accountability of the government. Marc Chernick (1991) suggests that the exclusive nature of Colombia's National

Front government between 1958 and 1974 led to the emergence of insurgent groups in subsequent years.

In response to these criticisms, Lijphart refers to the consociational arrangement as not an institutional blueprint but a set of *principles* to which certain institutions—such as a proportional representation electoral system—are naturally suited. For example, he replies to the charge that consociationalism can "freeze" or rigidify segments by arguing that a proportional representation electoral system allows the segments to "define themselves." While the institutions of consociational decision making vary, its advocates argue, the principles are rediscovered time and time again as societies seek solutions to the existence of intense ethnic politics and methods to harness ethnicity for constructive purposes.[17]

Power Sharing: The Integrative Approach

In contrast to the consociational model, Horowitz (1985:597–600) proposes a typology of five mechanisms aimed at reducing ethnic conflict: (1) dispersions of power, often territorial, which "proliferate points of power so as to take the heat off of a single focal point"; (2) devolution of power and reservation of offices on an ethnic basis in an effort to foster intraethnic competition at the local level; (3) inducements for interethnic cooperation, such as electoral laws that effectively promote preelection electoral coalitions through vote pooling; (4) policies to encourage alternative social alignments, such as social class or territory, by placing political emphasis on crosscutting cleavages; and (5) reducing disparities between groups through managed distribution of resources.

Horowitz's prescriptions for conflict-regulating institutions in divided societies overlap those of Lijphart in certain respects: both advocate federalism, for example, and assert the importance of proportionality and ethnic balance. Yet Horowitz is an indefatigable critic of the consociational model for two important reasons (1985:568–576; 1991:137–145). First, he argues, is the problem of "elite-initiated conflict" that Tsebelis and Burg also identify. "There is no reason to think automatically," Horowitz writes, "that elites will use their leadership position to reduce rather than pursue conflict" (1991:141). Consociationalism overestimates the deference communal groups pay to their leaders and underestimates the power and role of popular dissatisfaction with intergroup compromise.

Second, consociational institutions rely on constraints against immoderate politics, such as the mutual or minority veto, versus incentives for moderation (1991:154–160). Horowitz argues that political institutions should encourage or induce integration across communal divides. For effective democratic governance in a divided society, moderates must be rewarded, extremists sanctioned. The aim is to engineer a *centripetal* spin to the political system by providing electoral incentives for broad-based moderation by political leaders and disincentives for extremist outbidding (1985:601–652). This idea differentiates Horowitz's prescriptions from those of consociationalism in two important respects.

First, the key to any successful democratic political system in divided societies is to provide demonstrable incentives for politicians to appeal beyond their own communal segments for support. The only assumption is this: politicians will do whatever they need to do to get elected; they are rational electoral actors (Horowitz 1991:261). When politicians are rewarded electorally for moderation, they temper their rhetoric and actions. Given this premise, the political system can be engineered to essentially encourage intergroup cooperation as a prerequisite for electoral success. Horowitz contends that incentives are better than consociational constraints (such as the mutual veto) because they offer *reasons* for politicians and divided groups to behave moderately, rather than *obstacles* aimed at preventing them from pursuing hegemonic, defeat-the-other aims.

The second difference is a concern with constituency-based moderation rather than reliance on political leaders as the engine of moderation. The solution is to design the electoral system so that leaders must appeal to underlying moderate sentiments in the electorate and shun the forces of extremism to win elections. Office seekers, by appealing to the most moderate sentiments of the electorate, maximize moderation at both the elite and the popular levels. Looking for the basis of consent at the constituency level allows politicians to make the kinds of compromises they must make at the center if the divided society is to be stable and truly democratic. The key to constituency-based moderation is the electoral system. To safeguard minority interests, according to Horowitz, the system should make the votes of minority members count. Minorities should have more than *representation*, they should have *influence*. Three institutions and practices are argued to have these effects: federalism, vote pooling, and the presidential system.

1. *Federalism.* Dramatic devolution of power can serve four important purposes in divided societies, according to Horowitz (1985:601). First, it can combine with the electoral system to encourage the party proliferation that is conducive to inter-segmental compromise and coalition building. Second, politics at the regional and local levels can serve as training grounds for politics at the center: political leaders can form intergroup ties at the constituency level before they contest higher-stakes issues at the level of central government. Third, federalism disperses conflict at the center by resolving some issues at subtier levels and, in communally homogeneous federal states, may promote cleavages *within* groups. Finally, it creates difficulties for any parties hoping to get a hegemonic grip on the entire country; capturing all of the provincial states would be a difficult task. For example, the adoption of federalism at the time of democratization in Spain is an instructive example of successful ethnic conflict management through devolution (Horowitz 1985:623; Share 1986). "Federalism can either exacerbate or mitigate ethnic conflict," Horowitz writes; "much depends on the number of components, the number of states, boundaries, and the ethnic composition" (1985:603).

2. *Vote pooling.* To Horowitz, divided societies need electoral systems that fragment support of one or more ethnic groups, especially ethnic majorities; induce interethnic bargaining; encourage the formation of multiethnic coalitions; produce fluidity and a multipolar balance; and produce proportional outcomes. Three types of electoral systems can achieve these

aims: a subsequent-preference voting system (among these systems, the preferable one is *alternative voting*); mixed lists with
a common voters roll; and single-member districts in multiethnic constituencies. In each instance the purpose is to promote vote pooling by candidates or parties across ethnic lines.
Although electoral systems and conflict management will be
more thoroughly discussed in chapter 4, a brief introduction
here highlights the differences between the consociational and
integrative approaches.

Why are electoral systems that provide for vote pooling
superior for divided societies, in Horowitz's view? The logic is
this: to win, politicians must seek to obtain the second- or
third-preference votes of those who would not ordinarily vote
for them (presumably because they do not represent the voter's
community). To gain second- or third-preference votes, leaders must behave moderately toward other communal groups.
Outbidding will inevitably occur, Horowitz agrees, but so too
will moderation. In response to the incentive structure of the
electoral system, most politicians will vie to appear the most
moderate—they will compete with one another to define and
occupy the political center. Centripetal forces will override
centrifugal ones. The critical difference between the consociational approach to electoral systems and Horowitz's is thus the
formation of electoral coalitions by constituents as they specify
their second or third preferences beyond their own narrow
group interests. As examples of successful interethnic vote
pooling, Horowitz (1993) cites the system established by the
Sri Lankan constitution of 1978, and the electoral politics of
the Indian state of Kerala, where four major ethnic blocs share
power in a fluid system of changing coalitions and alliances.

3. *The presidential system.* A presidency, argues Horowitz, if
elected directly on the basis of a super-majority distributional
formula or a subsequent-preference voting method, is a less
exclusive institution than parliamentarism. Presidentialism is
argued to have two important advantages in divided societies:
First, if a president is elected with an electoral system that

requires broadly distributed support, an executive who has the broadest possible national appeal can be elected. A strong, statesmanlike, moderate president—forced to appeal to the least common denominator of electoral sentiments—can serve a unifying, nation-building role (Horowitz 1990a). Second, a strong executive would be able to push legislation through a divided parliament. If strong but benevolent leadership is required—to make tough economic decisions or redress historical injustices, for example—a strong president is desirable. An example of such a presidential system, according to Horowitz, is Nigeria's (1985:636).

Horowitz's broad approach to ethnic conflict management—"the political incentive structure is one package," he writes (1985:651)—has also encountered criticism, considered here, as have the specific conflict-regulating practices (considered in chapter 4). There are four interrelated concerns: a paucity of empirical examples of the system at work; the questionable assumption that politicians will respond to the incentive system for moderation if it exists; that voters be willing to vote for parties not based in their own group; and that the electoral systems Horowitz advocates are essentially majoritarian. Like criticisms of consociationalism, these concerns go beyond simple conflict-regulating mechanisms and are rooted in basic beliefs about the fluidity and malleability of ethnic identity and representation.

The criticism that there are few empirical examples of the system at work is the most important. In response, Horowitz acknowledges that few countries have "full packages of all the right institutions, [which is] a wrong standard in an area where we are trying to divine innovations, wherever they may be found, for countries with a surplus of conflict and no obvious way out of it. If whole country explanations could be found, this would not be such a serious problem to begin with."[18] In chapter 4, the cases where integrative practices have been introduced are more fully explored.

At the heart of the difference between consociational and integrative approaches to power sharing are the nature and formation of multiethnic coalitions. In the consociational approach, coalitions are formed after an election by elites who realize that exclusive decision making will make the society ungovernable or who are compelled to do so by prior constitutional arrangements that are based on the same reasoning. In an integrative power-sharing system, coalitions are formed prior to an election—either as a coalition of parties in preelection pacts (vote pooling) or by a party with a broad multiethnic candidate slate. Consociational arrangements formed after elections, Horowitz contends, are fragile and tenuous "coalitions of convenience" as opposed to firm and enduring "coalitions of commitment" (1985:365–395).

4

A Typology of Conflict-Regulating Practices

A central argument of this book is that in the above-outlined debate neither approach can be said to be the best in all circumstances. Rather, the two approaches should be seen in contingent terms and in terms of a spectrum of options from the most consociational to the most integrative. The appropriate question is, Under what ethnic conflict conditions is the consociational approach likely to mitigate conflict, and under what conditions is an integrative approach likely to produce success? The challenge is not to develop a singular *model* of conflict-regulating practices, but rather a *menu* of conflict-regulating practices that disputants and mediators can choose from and adapt to the intricacies and challenges of successfully regulating any given ethnic conflict.

Eric Nordlinger's seminal 1972 study *Conflict Regulation in Divided Societies* identified six political methods and practices that account for successful conflict regulation in societies with deep ethnic fissures: (1) stable governing coalitions, (2) the principle of proportionality, (3) mutual veto, (4) purposive depoliticization, (5) compromises on key issues, and (6) concessions by conflict groups. These practices generally reflect the consociational vein of thinking about democracy in divided societies, relying principally on elite accommodation, popular deference to elites, group solidarity, and legitimate group representation. Given recent experiences with power sharing both successful and unsuccessful—and criticisms lodged against consociational and integrative approaches—it is possible to refine, build on, and expand Nordlinger's typology to encompass an amended and enlarged typology of conflict-regulating practices, including integrative practices.

The premise underlying an expanded list of options is that *in some instances the consociational approach may lead to successful conflict regulation, whereas in other instances an integrative approach may be best.* Which approach will contribute to success is highly dependent on the structure of ethnic relations, the specific patterns of ethnic politics in a given community, the historical development of a given conflict, the relationship between ethnic groups and the state, the attitudes and skills of political leaders, and the ability of groups in conflict to agree on the core principles underlying their political system.

In compiling a revised typology, I believe that the consociational and integrative approaches to power sharing can be presented as a broader menu of conflict-regulating practices and institutions. And, as is illustrated below, once a process of political change sets in—for example, a peace process or a transition to democracy, often two sides of the same coin—parties to a conflict choose different types of political practices and institutions on the basis of their own situational interests and goals.[1] That is, outcomes are "path dependent." Indeed, as Adam Przeworski argues, democracy evolves as a contingent outcome of conflicts (1988).

Successful conflict-regulating practices involve establishing a stable set of formal or informal rules and institutions that encourage political leaders and groups in conflict to behave moderately toward one another. When groups in conflict commit to a common set of rules and institutions, the structure of those institutions can make a difference in containing conflict along ethnic lines. In developing a typology of conflict-regulating practices and differentiating consociational practices from integrative practices, it is useful to consider the practices in terms of three sets of variables that apply to both approaches: territorial divisions of power, decision rules, and defining relations between the state and ethnic groups. The first two deal with constitutional structure, whereas the third relates to public policies.

Territorial Divisions of Power

When the territorial dimensions of ethnicity are strong, practices that *configure the territorial division of power* are exceptionally important. The range of options within these types of practices is between partition (separation) and a centralized unitary state (the ultimate form of sharing), with a variety of options such as confederal, federal, and semiconfederal systems in between. It is widely agreed that the territorial division of power can serve a variety of purposes beyond simple devolution, including providing economic mechanisms (such as for affecting the distribution of resources) and political mechanisms (such as reducing the stakes of conflict at the center).

Territorial boundaries can even be structured to straddle the fence between separation and power sharing. Examples are various recent proposals for confederations that have special linkages across international frontiers: a Palestinian-Jordanian confederation with lingering ties to Israel; the two territorial "entities" that form the basis of the recent Dayton, Ohio, agreement on postconflict Bosnia, in which a Bosnian Muslim and Bosnian Croatian entity would have special ties to Croatia while a Bosnian Serb entity would have ties to Serbia; and myriad plans for resolving the Northern Ireland dispute.[2]

Among the variety of methods for dividing territory, federalism is the most extensively analyzed for its potential conflict-regulating effects. Federalism, it should be noted, can be structured for either consociational or integrative purposes. Indeed, the opportunities for innovation are so extensive that federalism can be structured to serve both ends within a given state. In multiethnic societies, the test of federalism is the degree to which territorial units coincide with or are parallel with communal boundaries.[3] By promoting intraethnic conflict within each subnational territorial unit, federalism can potentially create incentives for interethnic cooperation, encourage alignments along nonethnic interests, and be fiscally structured to level socioeconomic disparities. Devolution of power can give minorities some degree of power when it is unlikely that they would ever achieve majority status at the center.[4]

The primary distinction in divided societies is between poly-communal federal structures, mixed federal structures, and non-communal federations (Duchacek 1973:166ff.). Polycommunal federations are systems in which internal territorial divisions closely correspond to the major ethnic, linguistic, religious, or racial groupings; examples include the former Soviet Union, the former Czechoslovakia, and Burma. Mixed federations combine some territorial self-government based on ethnic interests with other territorial units that are essentially heterogeneous; examples include Canada, the former Yugoslavia, and India. Still other federations, notably the U.S. system, have no ethnic base to their federal structure. The paramount issue in divided societies is the relationship between the spatial distribution of ethnic groups and the territorial distribution of the states. Do they overlap or cut across communal boundaries?

Federalism implies a division of power based on mutual consent. The national or central government is bestowed with a defined area of authority, the territorial units are provided degrees of autonomy, and both tiers of government enjoy some limited coordinated powers.[5] The hallmark of federalism is that neither the center nor the regions can amend the arrangement without mutual consent (Wheare 1964:xviii). It is through federal structures that the principle of unity through diversity, an essential norm of democracy in divided societies, can best be realized; this is especially true with respect to the protection of minorities through a panoply of options such as grants of autonomy, indigenous rights, and semisovereign ancestral lands, and recognition of limited territorial self-determination (Hannum 1990).[6] The salutary effects of federalism can sometimes be enhanced with a superlocal option, giving maximum autonomy to localized units such as Switzerland's cantons. In this vein, creative options for managing large, multiethnic cities may be required even as relatively homogeneous rural areas are granted a high degree of autonomy.

There are costs associated with federalism, such as the resource drain created by parallel government structures on many levels and the constant tensions over jurisdiction. Most important, ill-structured federalism may lead to secession. As many parties to conflict and many policymakers readily understand, the most serious danger inherent in federalism is the potential of creating fissiparous tendencies by giving territorially concentrated ethnic groups a base from which to withdraw or even secede from the common polity. A clear and present danger in many federal systems is the territorializing of ethnicity, possibly creating incentives for secession or autonomy. When smaller subunits are likely to also contain minority groups, the problems of divided societies are deferred but not solved by ill-devised federal schemes. How many subdivisions of the state are required before the elusive goal of a homogeneous state is reached? Clearly, the current experiment in Ethiopia—which has adopted the principle of "ethnic federalism"—will test the ability of that society to maintain a precarious balance between unity and diversity.[7]

Ethnic federalism was the basis of the structure of the republics in the former Soviet Union—where republics were based on titular nationalities to resolve the national question—whose constitution (Article 72) clearly provided for the right to secede. The lessons from federalism in the former Soviet Union are twofold: first, federalism without a devolution of power is no federalism at all; and second, strict national federalism can potentially lead to disintegration. Manipulative boundary delimitation in the former Soviet Union complicated ethnic relations (for example, between Armenia and Azerbaijan), and its legacy is still felt today in continuing conflicts over boundaries, citizenship, and the status of autonomous and semiautonomous regions within the Russian Federation. Similarly, colonial policy on the territorial division of power in Nigeria and Sudan left a legacy of conflict in these states, both of which have suffered (or in the case of Sudan, continue to suffer) from secessionist armed struggles (Rothchild 1995). For federalism or regionalism to unify, not divide, the polity, it must be coupled with policies whose effect is to raise the cost of a successful secession and increase the benefits of association.

A preeminent example of federalism as a conflict-regulating practice is India, whose complex system of twenty-two states and nine union territories is based on a combination of heterogeneous states and linguistically determined boundaries—a remnant of colonial expansion. The Indian constitution recognizes the diversity of the country's languages as the most persistent and important social cleavage, but the diversity has been contained through a combination of sound policy (establishing national and regional official languages, for example), an overriding consensus in favor of accommodation (Nariman 1989:7–37; Das Gupta 1989:63ff.), and the use of force against secessionist movements.

While India's track record on successfully managing intercommunal conflicts is at best mixed, and it has by no means fully resolved the social inequalities of race, caste, and religion, its federal system is useful for comparative analysis because of its balance of cohesive and diverse states combined with a history of a dominant and relatively inclusive nationalist party (Congress) at the center. India has been widely regarded as the prime example of successful integrative practices in a divided society. It has survived as the world's largest democracy, and yet its model of governance conforms remarkably close to the typical Westminster-style majoritarian system. Brass (1990) suggests that India's experience alone places in question the claims by consociationalists that democracy in a multiethnic society is impossible within a majoritarian framework. Lijphart, however, contends that India had elements of consociational power sharing until the 1960s and that the diminution of power-sharing practices has led to the increasing fragility of India's political system (1994b).

India's rising communal strife—evidenced by religious violence between Hindu and Muslim communities, the costly secessionist struggle in Kashmir, and the simmering unrest in Punjab, Assam, and (more recently) Tamil Nadu—exemplifies the difficulty of maintaining a unified democracy among a diverse population. Without federalism and a history of flexibility in redesigning the territorial boundaries of states, however, India might well have disintegrated long ago. As Hardgrave (1994) suggests, federalism in India has helped "compartmentalize friction."

A persistent problem with federalism is to resolve questions of dual sovereignty. Which unit—central or federal—has sovereign power over various functions of state? Although this problem vexes nearly every federation, the problem can be addressed with pragmatism. For example, looser federations may give subnational units some degree of control over foreign affairs, as Russia has granted Tatarstan functional flexibility in its external relations. Like other conflict-regulating practices, federalism is highly flexible. As new territorial units are created, so too are opportunities for innovative practice. Six of India's states, for example, have adopted the use of ombudsmen; many have complex language policies to meet local ethnic demands. For this reason, federalism offers innumerable opportunities for addressing the absolute complexity of ethnic demands in deeply divided societies within a democratic framework. For complex multiethnic states in the developing world, as Richard Sklar (1987:698) writes, "federalist futures are democratic images."

Decision Rules

As Douglas Rae has observed, the crux of decision making within a democracy is the threshold of consensus required for some members of the society to take decisions that apply to all members of society (Rae 1969). Thus, practices are critical that establish rules whereby executive and legislative decisions are made by elites and representatives are selected by the electorate (the electoral system). Options exist between minimum winning decision rules (for example, a plurality) to complete consensus.

Executive, Legislative, and Administrative Structures

There is a long-standing debate between advocates of parliamentary government and advocates of presidential executives as to which system is more inherently stable and inclusive.[8] In a typical parliamentary system, the executive is drawn from the ranks of parliamen and ultimately dependent on its members for its continued governance. In coalition governments, the leader of the largest party in the parliament serves as prime minister, and the cabinet is drawn from the majority party or parties. In grand coalitions, sometimes known as governments of national unity or national fronts, all significant political parties are represented in a ruling coalition and participate in executive decision making. Cabinet posts are doled out carefully and with an eye toward a balance of power commensurate with each party's electoral strength, creating a plural executive. Decisions are made by consensus, with each segment exercising a mutual veto.

Parliamentary structures are attractive options for divided societies, because they may be structured to facilitate the inclusion of many groups, including minorities, at the highest levels of government, for instance, in a broadly representative cabinet. Juan Linz (1990:72) argues that parliamentary systems "are more conducive to stable democracy" than presidential systems and that this point "applies especially to nations with deep political cleavages and numerous political parties." Parliamentary government, he contends, allows for many shades of possible political outcomes; when combined with a variable term (the government can be forced to resign when majority parliamentary support is withdrawn), it is a highly flexible arrangement. Presidential systems—with executive branch authority highly centralized in one individual who is usually, but not always, directly elected—are by definition more exclusive than parliamentary systems, particularly if the president is unambiguously identifiable as a member of any one community or interest.

The problem with a parliament-chosen executive, according to Horowitz (1990a:73–79), is that in typical parliamentary systems whichever party or coalition of parties has a bare majority in the legislature can choose an executive without regard to the preferences of the minority; when parliament-chosen executives fall in the winner-take-all, government-versus-opposition pattern of politics, an already divided society is further divided. A minimum winning coalition usually forms the government. Instead, Horowitz believes that a separately elected presidency combined with a strict separation of legislative and executive powers can proliferate points of power at the center, allowing some parties to win sometimes and others to win at other times. Dispersing power in a political system through a system of checks, balances, and divided responsibility lowers the stakes of control for any particular institution or office (the separation-of-powers doctrine). If the stakes are very high for any particular office or number of seats, conflict between winners and losers rises commensurately.

For Horowitz, a nationally elected president with exceptionally broad support is more likely to have conflict-reducing effects in a divided society than the parliamentary counterpart.[9] A presidential system can be constructed so as to ensure that in order to be elected, candidates must present themselves as conciliatory broad-based leaders. The provisions of the 1979 and 1989 constitutions of Nigeria illustrate. In Nigeria's Second Republic (1979 constitution), election to the presidency required the candidate to take due notice of the "federal character" of the state; to win, the candidate was required to garner a plurality of votes nationwide and at least 25 percent of the votes in thirteen of Nigeria's then nineteen states. In the Third Republic's constitution, promulgated by the Babangida military government (after a constitutional constituent assembly) in 1989, an even more stringent requirement was built into the constitution to require a "supermajority" for election to the presidency: "He has to have not less than one-third of the votes cast at the election in each of at least two-thirds of all the states in the Federation." In the event a single candidate does not meet this test in the first round of balloting, a runoff election is required. It was, however, a dispute over the 1983 presidential election that contributed in part (another cause was corruption in the civil service) to the downfall of the Second Republic (1979–1983).

A broad-minded individual fairly pursuing aims of national integration can serve a symbolically important conflict-reducing role. South Africa's Nelson Mandela, with broad public support and leading the country with an ethos of national reconciliation and moderation, is Horowitz's ideal president—in essence, standing above the ethnic fray. Although South Africa technically has a parliamentary system (the president is indirectly elected, and the system essentially allows for the majority party in parliament to elect its candidate president), Mandela's behavior as a president exemplifies the role a president can play. Critics of the supermajority requirement point out that there are, as Andrew Reynolds writes, "virtually no good examples of a president directly elected who becomes a unifying force in a divided society. Nigeria didn't work, and most super-majority systems fail as well. Either one group is large enough to surmount a 50 percent or 66 percent barrier, or no [candidate] gains the supermajority and the country is thrown into even more dangerous confusion."[10]

Executive structures, too, can be highly flexible and adaptable to circumstance. Creating a broad-based executive can be a voluntary move to promote a sense of security and inclusion for aggrieved groups, or it can be statutorily or constitutionally mandated. Often it is simply politically pragmatic, enhancing the legitimacy of the government. And the decision rules adopted by inclusive or coalition governments can be created so as to ensure wide consensus before major policy decisions are made, without being so laborious that they prevent the regular exercise of executive power. For example, in the current transitional power-sharing government in South Africa, all parties that received at least 5 percent of the vote are entitled to a cabinet seat, and those that garnered 20 percent or more of the vote are entitled to a deputy president slot. Decisions are to be made with the broadest possible consensus, but complete unanimity is not required.

Broad-based executives are more easily created if the principle of proportionality is operational. Although this principle permeates many of the conflict-regulating practices identified here, the two most important proportionality practices are proportional representation in appointments, which often takes the form of the constitutionally entrenched reservation of offices on an ethnic or territorial basis, and a proportional representation electoral system.

Perhaps the best-known example of proportional appointments was the Lebanese National Pact of 1943, which mandated top posts for representatives of the Christian (Maronite), Druze, Shi'a, Sunni, and other communities. Seats may also be reserved in legislatures. In Indonesia, Chinese, Europeans, and Arabs are awarded 9, 6, and 3 seats in parliament, respectively, if as many are not duly elected.[11] For the first ten years of independence in Zimbabwe, 20 of the 100 seats in parliament were reserved for whites even though they constituted but 3 percent of the country's population. Nigeria's 1989 constitution stipulates that if the president comes from the North, the majority party leader must come from the South; Tanzania has similar arrangements.

Like many of the conflict-regulating practices, proportional appointments can be handled informally. For example, South Africa's new constitutional court is carefully balanced on many variables (ethnicity, gender, generation, region, race, language, and ideology) even though such proportionality is not strictly mandated in the constitution. Routine bureaucratic appointments can also be conducted in accordance with the proportionality principle. Indeed, although power sharing is mandated in the country's constitution, much of the real sharing of power in South Africa is conducted in an informal manner, and much of it within the broadly multiethnic ruling party, the African National Congress (ANC). As Donald Rothchild notes, "with the ANC supported by a very large majority, it only needs to concede formal power sharing for a very temporary period and largely to make whites feel secure so they will not discourage international investors. But the real power sharing takes place as much within the ANC itself (that is, among the factions) and between the ANC and white-led civil service and police."[12] Similarly, the nascent social partnership among business, labor, and the state in managing economic matters is an example of informal power sharing in the sphere of economic policy.

The most important appointments and offices are those in the security forces, for the military and the police are often the "ultimate arbiters" of social relations in divided societies (Esman 1994:228). It is no surprise that in many instances of ethnic group domination, the composition of the security forces is a continually contentious issue. Thus, perhaps the most critical regulatory practice in deeply divided societies is an integrated security force. For example, Burundi's army has an overwhelming majority of Tutsis although this group comprises only about 14 percent of the overall population. Changing the complexity of the security force structure is a delicate maneuver, fraught with potential pitfalls. Attempted reforms to achieve a more balanced representation of Hutu and Tutsi in Burundi's army led to the attempted coup in October 1992 that helped plunge the country into the current round of ethnic bloodletting. The composition of the security forces will be an important long-term issue in Northern Ireland as well, where 87 percent of the security force is drawn from the Protestant community, a result not of official discrimination in recruitment policies but of the unwillingness of Catholics to serve (Boyle and Hadden 1994:47).

Other problems with proportional communal representation arise when the structure is unresponsive to demographic changes in the underlying population. At least one factor in the 1975 collapse of the Lebanese National Pact of 1943 was the demographic shift as the Christian majority population became a minority. The deterioration of Lebanon into one of the world's intractable civil wars between 1976 and 1990 attests to the dangers of such rigidity.[13] Whether the National Pact can be labeled a success (for mediating conflict for more than thirty years) or a failure (because it degenerated into civil war) is an open question. In many ways it was both.

It is significant that in the 1990 Lebanese constitution the formulas for representation have been changed. Seats in the National Assembly are allocated on a half-Moslem, half-Christian basis with further sub-group sectarian and regional representation. However, the 1989 Taif Accord that led to the new constitution stipulates that the eventual electoral law will wholly remove inflexible guarantees for sectarian representation. Joseph Maila notes that the Taif Accord "recognizes that confessionalism is a regulating principle of political society by claiming that power cannot be legal if it contravenes the 'Pact of Co-existence' or the 'desire to live together' (*al aysh al-mushtarik*)" (1992:17).

Choosing an Appropriate Electoral System

An appropriate electoral system in a divided society is arguably the most important mechanism through which parties in conflict can adopt a democratic conflict-regulating practice. This is true because, as Giovanni Sartori has written, electoral systems are "the most specific manipulative element of politics" (1968:273).[14] The debate over which electoral system is best is complicated because electoral system design can be a very technical matter; the outcomes that flow from a specific choice are highly dependent on unknowns such as the spatial distribution of votes, shifting party alignments and inter-party pacts, voting behavior, ballot design, and myriad other variables. Moreover, formal theorists have shown that no single system is arguably the "fairest" because of the "paradox of voting"; with the same set of voter preferences, different systems yield different winners (Arrow 1963). Finally, electoral system choices inevitably involve trade-offs among values such as legitimacy, simplicity, accountability, and proportionality.

For deeply divided societies the central issue is, What is best: the majoritarian system, the less demanding plurality systems, or some type of proportional representation system? Underlying the debate is the clear understanding that electoral system choice eventually has a strong effect on the type of party system that emerges (Lijphart 1994a); plurality and majoritarian systems tend to produce two-party systems, whereas proportional representation usually leads to a fragmented multiparty system (Duverger 1964). In this regard the policy-relevant differences between the consociational and integrative approaches to power sharing are most acute.

Advocates of consociationalism are strong believers in simple systems of proportional representation (PR) that allow all parties (presumably, but not necessarily, ethnically based) representation in government commensurate with their share of the electorate. PR is not a single system but instead a broad *set* of electoral systems that seek to minimize differences between votes and seats in parliamentary elections (Taagepera and Shugart 1989:24–25).[15] By directly translating the number of votes won to the proportion of seats, PR systems are arguably more suited to providing incentives for including minority parties (Dahl 1989:156–162). The benefits of simple PR (especially *list-system* PR, in which parties offer slates of candidates), according to Lijphart, include a more precise vote-to-seat ratio; the lack of "wasted votes"; the ability of ethnic groups to "define themselves" and to achieve representation by their own leaders in legislative and executive institutions (Lijphart 1990a:10); immunity to gerrymandering;[16] and the likelihood that fragmentation of the party system will eventually result in coalition governments.

Opting for PR incurs the risk that the system may in fact provide incentives for social fragmentation. While PR may produce proportionality and allow for the politics of ethnic inclusion, the prospect of at least some presence in parliament (and of a parliamentary salary) can make it attractive for politicians to factionalize into narrowly based, exclusive parties, a phenomenon that Sartori (1966) has termed "polarized pluralism."[17] The proliferation of parties during the continually troubled Weimar republic led postwar constitutional designers in Germany to adopt a threshold for representation (5 percent), a common practice now in PR systems. In circumstances of fragile minimum winning coalitions, such as in Israel, small parties can hold the balance of power in potentially destabilizing ways by weakening government and forcing onto the agenda narrow interests or highly volatile ethnic issues.

Horowitz, on the other hand, sees advantages to PR under certain specific conditions (1985:628–653), but the *purposes* of electoral system design are different from those proposed by Lijphart. In addition to achieving proportionality and reducing disproportionate vote-to-seat ratios, Horowitz suggests, the effects of the electoral system should also be to fragment support for ethnic parties; induce an ethnic group, particularly a majority group, to behave moderately; preserve fluidity and multipolar balance to prevent exclusion; and, most important, encourage preelection coalitions of parties across ethnic cleavages or, if possible, the creation of broad multiethnic parties (1985:632).

Although Horowitz agrees that simple list-system PR can be structured to meet these goals, he identifies problems with it, namely, the strong role played by party bosses; representatives' lack of a constituency link; a lack of accountability; the potential incentives contained in the system for the proliferation of ethnic parties and ethnic outbidding; and the lack of incentives for cross-group integration. He and other integrationists (for example, Lardeyret [1991]) argue that the electoral system should root accommodation across group lines at both the elite and the popular levels in society and should seek to integrate groups into large multiethnic parties. On the other hand, large multiethnic parties are criticized for being a mask for ethnic dominance, in which the votes of some minorities are taken for granted given the electorate's choices (for example, black votes for the Democratic Party in the United States).

To meet the integrative aims he sets out, Horowitz favors vote pooling as a mechanism for inducing moderation; vote pooling systems provide opportunity for voters to cast not only their first-preference votes but subsequent-preference votes as well. In providing examples of vote pooling, Horowitz (1985, 1991) favorably cites the *alternative-vote* system (parties can agree to pool votes) or the *single-transferable-vote* system (candidates can make vote-pooling agreements); second- and third-preference votes can be transferred among candidates or parties in a complex computation that produces overall winners.[18] Lijphart (1991) counters that alternative-vote electoral systems are no better and sometimes worse than simple majoritarian electoral systems and that vote pooling can be achieved in many variants of list PR, primarily through the system of *apparentement* (in which parties can link their candidate lists). The major preconditions for a successful vote-pooling framework are sufficient party proliferation, large heterogeneous constituencies, and conditions that make vote pooling profitable: that is, the second- and third-preference votes political leaders gain from being moderate on communal interests outnumber the first-preference votes they lose by appearing soft.[19]

Neither Nigeria nor Sri Lanka, the principal cases Horowitz relies on to make the argument for the salutary effects of vote pooling, have had their electoral systems fully tested. Other examples such as Kerala (in India) are of limited comparative value given the idiosyncratic context of regional politics within overall national politics in India. Nevertheless, these examples do show that innovative solutions are conceivable to create an electoral system that provides incentives for intergroup moderation. Crawford Young writes, "In Malaysia, the semi-consociational management of racial divisions has probably been facilitated by the operation of the plurality system which in this setting provided incentives for co-operation within the

Malay-dominated ruling alliances, whose electoral majority is magnified by the Westminster model" (1995:12).[20]

The problem, of course, is the difficulty of winning support across group boundaries in situations of deep conflict. Nordlinger anticipates the problem when he writes that "even if party leaders were to mitigate their positions on the less salient issues, members of the opposing conflict group are not likely to change their party attachments on the basis of a secondary issue" (1972:102). Horowitz notes that the only assumption behind the successful operation of a vote-pooling framework "is that voters will vote for candidates other than those of their own group if advised to do so by leaders of the ethnic party they support (and usually only for second preferences). There is abundant evidence from Malaysia that they do this regularly, and it does not depend on the malleability of ethnic identity or even a softening of conflict."[21] In situations where the population is highly illiterate or innumerate, however, these systems may simply be too complicated, especially when severe conflict places a premium on clearly legitimate and simply understood election results.

Although vote-pooling is theoretically compelling, there is simply insufficient empirical evidence at the level of national politics to support claims that subsequent-preference voting can lead to accommodative outcomes; the converse, however, is also true, suggesting that experimentation (for example, running election data under different rules) might yield further insights into the applicability of these systems to serve as a conflict-regulating device. Andrew Reynolds, for example, has "rerun" the 1994 elections in South Africa and Malawi under alternative electoral rules, finding proportional representation to have been generally more inclusive than plurality electoral systems (Reynolds, forthcoming).

Electoral systems are highly flexible and can be pieced together in many ways to be appropriate for specific conditions. For example, given large heterogeneous electoral districts, it may be possible to create a simple PR list system that gives parties incentives to put up multiethnic slates—an integrative practice—to maximize support. When large multimember constituencies are ethnically diverse and no single group dominates, a party seeking to maximize its vote share would want to appeal as broadly as possible and thus moderate its ethnic themes during an election campaign. In this manner, list PR can achieve integrative aims by providing incentives for coalitions of different variations within a single party, as was the case with the choice for PR in South Africa's first all-race elections (Sisk 1995a). In a subsequent analysis of the April 1994 vote in South Africa, I suggest that parties did in fact respond to the incentives imbedded in the electoral system to moderate their campaign rhetoric and that the top two vote getters (the ANC and the National Party) deliberately structured their candidate lists to appear racially inclusive (Sisk 1995b).

Moreover, the simple form of PR provided an incentive for potential spoilers of the election, whose boycott or violent opposition to the poll would have severely undermined the legitimacy of the vote and precipitated a broader crisis, to join the electoral bandwagon at the last minute, aware that even if they had no prospect of a majority of seats in parliament, they would gain sufficient representation to serve in the government of national unity.[22] A last-minute concession to allow for a double ballot (one national vote, one regional), designed to placate the regionally strong Inkatha Freedom Party, contributed to the conflict-ameliorating properties of this choice.

Thus, PR was a seemingly appropriate choice for this transitional or founding election and may be a good choice for other elections that are the culmination of a negotiated transition from deep conflict. Yet the South African system will likely be changed, because large multimember-district PR systems arguably lack accountability. For that reason, it is likely that South Africa will adopt a hybrid system similar to Germany's combination of national PR plus majoritarian single-member districts, a system that has contributed to stable electoral outcomes in the postwar era in that country (Kaase 1986). In the current deliberations over a more permanent electoral system for South Africa, there is a keen awareness that the system should try to maximize proportionality, incentives for moderation, representivity, and accountability.

Public Policy: Defining State-Ethnic Relations

Practices that *define relationships between ethnic groups and the state* are an essential dimension of conflict-regulating practices. At one end of a spectrum are practices that do not name specific groups or specify group rights or preferences in ethnic terms; on the other are those that enumerate and recognize special rights or preferences and confer them on distinct ethnic groups. Economic policies, the allocation of public funds, education and language policy, the delineation of rights and duties, the formulation of groups' rights when groups are entrenched, citizenship, and procedures of administering justice are all critical components of successful ethnic conflict management.

Crawford Young, in summarizing the findings of a United Nations Research Institute for Social Development study of public policies in ethnically diverse societies, writes, "Few if any state policies will be absolutely neutral in their distributive effects among ethnic groups. What matters, then, is whether the ethnic distributive effect is widely perceived as a product of deliberate bias towards those groups with favored access to the state," and whether offsetting policies are undertaken to redress the resulting imbalance (Young 1995:21).

Thus, conflict-regulating practices in divided societies have a significant "political economy" component.[23] If a source of ethnic conflict is the maldistribution of resources, what sorts of practices can lead to the appropriate redistribution of wealth or income? Kenneth McRae (1974) refers to a host of options as "fiscal equalization devices," that is, measures that promote the equitable distribution of society's resources. Such practices might include directed public policies, labor market policies, and differential access to certain resources. But as Esman (1994:239) notes, "excursion into economic variables demonstrates how difficult it is to explain or predict the effects of economic trends on ethnic-based conflict."

When ethnic groups have been historically disadvantaged or discriminated against, provisions have often been included—for example, in the United States, Sri Lanka, South Africa, India, and Pakistan—to acknowledge problems of discriminatory inequality.

Often, constitutional provisions do not spell out the public policy strategies to ameliorate the effects of past discrimination or comparative inequality but make the important symbolic statement that the aim of the polity is to seek redistribution. Enshrining the objective of uplifting those who may be disadvantaged can help chart the subsequent course of politics toward that end.

Perhaps the most striking example of such a commitment is the passage in the 1949 Indian constitution that declares, "The State shall promote with special care the educational and economic interests of the weaker sections of the people, and in particular, of the Scheduled Castes and the Scheduled Tribes, and shall protect them from social injustice and all forms of exploitation."[24] The implementation of affirmative action for historically disadvantaged groups in India, which is an effort to deal with the discriminatory effects of the caste system, has had a long and controversial past. Affirmative action in India has been criticized for perpetuating a sense of self-denigration among the disadvantaged groups and for its lack of effectiveness in eradicating inequality and discrimination (Nariman 1989:7). Most recently, it has been the cause of widespread violence among young upper-caste Indians who see their own futures jeopardized by such policies. As Diamond and Plattner (1994:xxvii) assert, India's experience (as well as Nigeria's) points out how "inflexible quotas for disadvantaged groups can actually reinforce group consciousness and generate explosive grievances by those groups that view themselves as victims of reverse discrimination." The debate over such policies in India in some ways mirrors the debate in other multiethnic societies, such as the United States (where such policies are being rolled back) and South Africa (where they are being increasingly implemented). Societies such as Rwanda, where patterned discrimination is still a serious problem, will eventually have to face this issue if longer-term conflict management is to occur.

Even though the problem of inequality in India is still very acute and high levels of inequality are tolerated, recognizing the disparity and committing state policy to resolving it is an important step in the right direction. In many instances, words are not met with deeds. While public policy goals of eradicating extreme disparities among groups are not always a constitutional phenomenon, in places with a historical pattern of oppression, such as caste-based oppression in India or race-based oppression in South Africa, expressing in the constitution the goal of eradicating the disparity can serve conflict-regulating ends. The 1990 constitution of Namibia (where apartheid was implemented during South Africa's occupation) sets forth goals for state policies that detail the objectives of state policies without making specific practices adjudicable in constitutional terms.[25]

Often the answer to such vexing problems is not to specify their solution in constitutional terms but to set up new institutions and procedures that all groups can subscribe to and that address equalization measures in collaborative, problem-solving forums. South Africa's new land restitution commission and court, whose establishment has defused and constructively channeled tensions, is an example worth considering for replication in other conflicts where land disputes are a central cause of continued hostilities.

One important conflict-regulating practice often ignored by power-sharing theorists, or at least downplayed, is the role of human rights (particularly the careful balancing of individual and group rights) and the role of judicial institutions in ethnic conflict mitigation. This is understandable, because courts are weak in most developing states. Legal protections for group rights, multiple official languages, own-language education, and special religious practices and customs; special statutory protection for named groups; and access to broadcast and print media may give groups comfort that their cultural identity is secure within a multiethnic framework. The self-management of community institutions and associations, that is, nonterritorial self-determination (sometimes known as *corporate*, as opposed to *territorial*, federalism), may be a sufficiently reassuring practice that groups will not seek other types of privileges or special representation.

A critical issue in divided societies is the careful balancing of individual and group rights and their adjudication. Courts and judges can reinforce political institutions and electoral practices as a final line of defense against despotic government, or they can be powerful weapons for the ethnically exclusive regime. Courts have sometimes shown extraordinary resilience in protecting ethnic minorities in the face of political pressure, as Zimbabwe illustrates (Sklar 1985:29–33). Innovations in judicial processes, such as the use of ombudsmen, can also serve to disperse power, protect rights, and address grievances. While these quasi-judicial officers are in use in few countries, the practice is innovative and deserves to be considered in deeply divided societies seeking novel solutions. Ombudsmen can provide a course of immediate and direct action for those who have been subject to discrimination or persecution.

The problem of constructing judicial institutions in divided societies has been addressed through creative solutions. In Nigeria, for example, the more than 26 million believers in Islam have pressed for access to the Islamic judicial system—the Shari'a courts—in matters of social and religious concern to them. This issue has also been central to the intense and ongoing conflict in Sudan. Nigeria's 1989 constitution allows states to establish Shari'a courts of appeal with jurisdiction in civil proceedings where both plaintiff and defendant are Muslim and agree to the court's review. In societies deeply divided by religious differences, such as Sudan and Nigeria, pragmatic solutions such as these may make the difference between relatively peaceful management of tensions or intractable war, even in the absence of a democratic framework.

The protection of rights—and increasingly the protection of minority rights—has traditionally been perceived as the telos of modern constitutionalism: the principle of *garantisme* (Sartori 1962) against arbitrary rule. In divided societies the issue has been whether there should be fully articulated rights to address minority group concerns. Such claims often take the form of demands for linguistic freedoms, particularly the right to education in one's mother tongue, the right to establish cultural and religious institutions or associations, protection against discrimination, and in some cases the right to self-determination. Some international law scholars assert strongly the case for further codification of minority rights; Hannum (1989:19) writes, "The essential philosophical underpinnings of human rights include the right to be and to live in community with other members of one's own group."

Clearly the protection of individual rights—including the rights of religious expression, free speech and association, freedom from discrimination, and a host of other political and civil rights—goes a long way in protecting the rights of national minorities. Whether such assurances should go so far as the failed Meech Lake Accord in Canada, which sought to constitutionally designate Quebec a "distinct society," are dubious. The Canadian Charter of Rights and Freedoms, adopted in 1982, sought to protect individual rights and, in doing so, to protect against discrimination as a member of a distinctive group. Meech Lake, on the other hand, undermined that liberal tradition by redefining Quebec in group rights terms as a distinct society. The dissolution of the Meech Lake and, later, the Charlottetown process in Canada shows that granting minority rights can have the effect of raising other claims, such as those of the Cree Indians, and may cause the constitutional basis of the state to weaken, precipitating a broader crisis (Welsh 1993:51).

Related to the notion of group rights is the opposite approach, specifically outlawing ethnic organizations, parties, or institutions. Although states cannot simply legislate away the structure of social alignments, some have tried. While such practices to reorient social alignments are few, those that have been pursued deserve careful consideration. The 1989 Constitution of Nigeria, for example, expressly forbids appeals by political leaders to ethnic solidarity, so that (it is hoped) they will define their political agendas in terms of ideology, class, or territory. The constitution explicitly states that a *political* objective of the state is to foster alternative social alignments; or, in the terms of Article 16 (d), to "promote or encourage the formation of associations that cut across ethnic, linguistic, religious, or other sectional boundaries."[26]

Opponents of statutory prohibitions against ethnic associations and parties suggest that prophylactic measures such as these will not prevent the creation of ethnic organizations but will push ethnic organizations outside the political system. Ethnic parties in divided societies are the principal means of securing ethnic interests. When the creation of broadly inclusive multiethnic parties is impossible, prohibiting ethnic parties makes accommodation impossible. In

Africa, where attempts to ban ethnic parties have been most frequent, Pearl Robinson writes, "One of the functions of parties is interest representation. And to the extent that issues of race, ethnicity, region, religion and gender are important to people, the banishment of these interests from formal and legitimate channels of political representation will not make them go away. In fact, misguided efforts to keep identity politics off the political agenda will actually fan the fires of alienation and revolt" (1995).

Ethnic politics is inextricably the politics of symbolism, and in this respect the state's practices can affect social alignments. Questions such as the status of language, so critical in nearly all divided societies, is often the most contested symbol. It is often perceived by disadvantaged groups as a stark symbol of domination. Some states (for example, India and Uganda) have resolved the highly charged and immensely symbolic language issues by turning to an alternative federal lingua franca, such as English. Language policies also have important ramifications for education and job opportunities for individuals. Other important national symbols, such as the official colors, flag, anthem, crest, and currency, must be perceived as neutral in divided societies if they are to serve the purpose of reorienting loyalty from ethnic groups to a common national state.[27]

Ten Conflict-Regulating Practices

From the discussion above, it is clear that any menu of conflict-regulating practices will be quite broad and that practices must fit together like a grand puzzle that, when pieced together, carefully meets a divided society's particular needs. With this proviso in mind, it is possible to discern ten distinct practices for conflict management that either embody a consociational or an integrative approach to ethnic conflict management. Some practices can serve either consociational or integrative aims, depending on how they are conceived and structured. Presented with the conflict-regulating practices are some hypotheses about their applicability under different conditions; some of the important issues that arise with their application are raised. Table 2 provides a summary.

Table 2. Conflict-Regulating Practices

	Consociational approach	Integrative approach
Territorial divisions of power	Granting autonomy and creating confederal arrangements	Creating a mixed or noncommunal federal structure
	Creating a polycommunal federation	Establishing a single inclusive unitary state
Decision rules	Adopting proportional representation and consensus rules in executive, legislative, and administrative decision making	Adopting majoritarian but integrated executive, legislative, and administrative decision making
	Adopting a highly proportional electoral system	Adopting a semimajoritarian or semi-proportional electoral system
State-ethnic relations	Acknowledging group rights or corporate federalism	Adopting ethnicity-blind public policies

Consociational Practices: Territorial Divisions of Power

1. *Granting autonomy and creating confederal arrangements.* Territorially concentrated ethnic groups, particularly minority groups, can be accommodated through grants of autonomy. Agreements are reached between the rump government and the autonomous units over issues such as economic and foreign relations and regional commerce. Decisions on these limited issues are made jointly. Critical variables are the degree of economic interdependence, the structure of fiscal relations, and the balance of dependency.

2. *Creating a polycommunal federation.* Territorially concentrated ethnic groups can also be accommodated in a polycommunal federation, that is, through "ethnic federalism." Ethnic federations require more extensive interaction than confederations at the central government level, and the allocation of powers between the central and regional governments is invariably a difficult and ongoing balancing act. Management of the economy and of the distribution of commonly held resources (for example, water, mineral rights) is critically important. Other thorny issues in constructing ethnic federations are boundary delimitation; the structure of security; the containment of secessionist tendencies; relations between subunits and foreign governments and international organizations; disparities across region or state in the adjudication of law, language, and education policy; and—perhaps most important—the status of minorities and majorities within any given region.

Consociational Practices: Decision Rules

3. *Adopting proportional representation and consensus rules in executive, legislative, and administrative decision making.* When all groups demand an influential role in decision making at various levels, proportional representation in the executive (through grand coalitions), the legislative (through the minority veto), and the administrative (through appointments) can serve conflict-

mitigating aims. The principle underlying such practices is consensus decision making. Such practices work best when there are few clearly identifiable groups and where disadvantaged groups have historically been excluded. Problems may arise when consensus is impossible or difficult to achieve and when any one group's leaders perceives it advantageous to act as a spoiler (withdrawing from participation and violently opposing accommodating groups). The most critical question is whether positions are reserved on the basis of statutorily defined groups or on the basis of electoral outcomes.

4. *Adopting a highly proportional electoral system.* Proportional representation electoral systems are useful for defining group boundaries where they are ambiguous or where an ethnic party competes against multiethnic parties. Moreover, these electoral systems (particularly list PR) can serve as the basis for determining the relative weight of various groups in terms of proportional representation in executive, legislative, and administrative arenas, especially when census data are inaccurate, suspicious, or absent. A critical issue is whether a simple PR system is expected to fragment the party system over time and what the implications of such fragmentation may be. A second issue is the appreciation that PR systems may not mitigate the effects of majority domination when the majority bloc is sufficiently cohesive.

Consociational Practices: State-Ethnic Relations

5. *Acknowledging group rights or corporate federalism.* When ethnic groups receive autonomy over issues that concern them most, such as language rights, state-financed own-language education, protection for cultural or religious activities, and access to customary law, they can feel sufficiently protected to participate in a common polity without fear that their identity will be subsumed in the overarching national ethos. Group rights may also amount to group preferences, particularly for historically disadvantaged groups. When an ethnic group is not territorially

concentrated, nonterritorial or corporate federalism can be introduced through the structure of group rights. However, group rights (especially preferences) can be difficult to adjudicate and can precipitate demands by other groups that may be more difficult to accommodate and that may provoke a backlash from nonpreferenced groups. Group rights and principles of individual equality are in constant tension.

Integrative Practices: Territorial Divisions of Power

6. *Creating a mixed or noncommunal federal structure.* When groups are not territorially concentrated, or when the aim of federalism is to promote intragroup cleavages and foster alignments across groups, a mixed or polycommunal federal approach may serve conflict-mitigating aims. Mixed federations are appropriate when one or two ethnic groups are mobilized, aggrieved, and territorially concentrated but other groups are more integrated; those territorially concentrated groups can be given special status or recognition while a nonethnic hue is preserved for the remainder of the polity. Noncommunal federalism can be especially appropriate when groups are not territorially concentrated or where significant minority communities will reside in all of the subunits. Dangers occur in mixed federations when special status is conferred on one territory but not others, and in noncommunal federations when some groups strive for greater territorial autonomy and such autonomy is not forthcoming.

7. *Establishing a single inclusive unitary state.* In some situations, it may be best to avoid the territorial division of power by working at the central and local government levels to develop conflict-regulating practices. In small states, states where economic integration is especially high, and states where grants of autonomy will lead to violent secessionist attempts, it may be best to centralize power but exercise it equitably. Unitary states are useful when a well-integrated elite exists and when efficient decision making is a premium, for example, to implement difficult structural adjustment economic policies.

Integrative Practices: Decision Rules

8. *Adopting majoritarian but integrated executive, legislative, and administrative decision making.* When political elites are integrated and when cleavages crosscut ethnic divisions, majoritarian decision making in the executive, legislative, and administrative fields is more efficient than reliance on consensus. Moreover, a host of integrative options are more demanding than simple majority rule but less demanding than consensus. The use of special majorities on key issues in both cabinet and legislative institutions (for example, through innovative parliamentary rules) can serve this aim without reliance on grand coalitions or minority vetoes for named groups. Inclusive, legitimate, and authoritative arbiters of conflict such as broadly accepted commissions and judicial bodies are good examples of integrated administrative decision-making practices.

9. *Adopting a semimajoritarian or semiproportional electoral system.* As a conflict-regulating practice, semimajoritarian electoral systems have traditionally been difficult to implement, but they nevertheless hold great promise. Electoral systems that are essentially majoritarian but that may, under certain conditions, have proportional effects (such as the alternative-vote system) or that are proportional but still have a majoritarian element (such as the single-transferable-vote system) advance conflict regulation by providing concrete incentives for candidate moderation across group lines. The principal problem with such systems is their complexity (either for voters or for understanding vote-to-seat formulae). However, sophisticated and complex electoral systems such as these may be effectively used in other decision-making fora, such as parliamentary elections for prime ministers or presidents.

If semimajoritarian or semiproportional systems can facilitate vote pooling, their conflict-regulating effects can be realized. In some instances, when group mutual security is of less particular concern, the plurality or simple majoritarian system is expected to be the most integrative electoral system. It should also be kept in mind that majoritarian and proportional systems can be combined, such as Germany's double ballot system. As with PR, a critical issue is how the electoral system relates to the territorial division of power.

10. *Adopting ethnicity-blind public policies.* When there is no particular pattern of historical inequality or no clear economic base to group mobilization, an ethnicity-blind public policy approach may serve integrative aims. When the rights of a group are protected through essentially individual rights (of association and nondiscrimination), group preferences can be avoided and the principle of individual equality can emerge as paramount. Practices such as adopting a lingua franca and eliminating ethnic traits in the overarching national identity are examples of such conflict-regulating practices.

The ten conflict-regulating practices identified here are offered as a general menu that, when applied, may well have different effects under different conditions. As in any engineering enterprise, there are risks of unanticipated consequences. Moreover, some of these practices—such as grand coalitions—are extraordinary measures that carry significant risk. When a party withdraws or threatens to withdraw from such a coalition as a tactical move to extract compromises from other parties, a constitutional crisis can easily be precipitated; coalition governments can mean chronic political instability. Precisely because many conflict-regulating practices are sometimes extraordinary and inefficient measures, it is important to consider under what conditions power sharing may be appropriate and when it can have adverse effects.

5

Power Sharing and Peace Processes

The principal assumption underlying power-sharing theory is the belief that appropriate political engineering can help construct a democratic political system capable of withstanding the centrifugal tendencies that tear deeply divided societies apart. Through constraints such as a mutual veto and incentives for cooperation such as a seat in the highest levels of government, power-sharing practices can arguably nudge ethnic groups and their leadership—given a basic commitment to a shared destiny and a common political home—to behave moderately toward one another and lead their communities to do so as well. This assumption, however, begs an important question: What are the incentives for the adoption of conflict-regulating practices? That is, Why would political leaders seek to create an often labyrinthine structure of democracy—with extraordinary measures such as a grand coalition—that is in many ways less efficient than the simply grasped majoritarian model?

Although the existing scholarship on power sharing offers excellent analysis of how such practices work, much less is known about how they come into being. Clearly they are linked to the processes of transition. Do stable democratic practices in multiethnic societies require a preexisting common political culture, or shared values? The experience with power sharing suggests that such a consensus need not exist, that a more minimalist set of conditions can lead to the adoption of appropriate conflict-regulating practices by parties to a conflict. A necessary condition is the realization by groups in conflict of a *shared or common destiny*, that is, an awareness of the essential reality that groups will in fact go on living together. A second necessary condition is the existence of pragmatic intergroup perceptions, a pragmatism that leads to collaborative problem solving through negotiation (that is, when negotiation is chosen not as a course through which to subdue the opponent, but for the purposes of jointly determining solutions).

Avoiding a Worse Outcome

What drives pragmatism in ethnic conflicts? Nordlinger (1972:42–53) identifies four motives that lead political leaders to accommodate: the existence of a common external threat; recognition that conflict distracts from economic well-being; the drive for power when incentives are so structured; and the avoidance of bloodshed or suffering. The last motive is arguably the most powerful. Desire for conflict avoidance has been termed by Lijphart the "self-negating prophecy": the belief that further escalation of violent conflict will not advance group aims but will in fact make them unattainable. Waterman (1993) argues that the need to control violence is the driving force that leads to negotiated settlements in civil wars.

Power-sharing practices often evolve as a direct response to a history of violent confrontation. The best example of a power-sharing pact emanating from a period of intense violence is Colombia (although the conflict was not ethnic). To end the strife known as *la Violencia*, the two principal parties agreed to forgo the polarizing effects of elections and rotate power for the next twenty years. The principal political parties reached a pact (the 1957 Pact of Sitges), which helped end seven years of fratricidal strife in which 200,000 lives were lost and which also paved the way for an end to military rule (Call 1995; Hartlyn 1988:60–61). The National Front power-sharing experiment in Colombia is generally perceived as a success, paving the way for an extended period of stability and economic expansion, although some (Chernick 1991) suggest that the rigidity and exclusiveness of the pact (power was shared by the two principal political parties) was a cause of insurgencies that developed in the mid-1980s.

The need to avoid violence goes a long way to explain why power sharing evolves in some situations. More difficult to explain are instances in which conflict leaders should readily appreciate the destructive nature of ethnic violence yet go on fomenting it nonetheless. Why do ethnic political and militia leaders in Burundi reject moderation when the costs of inflammatory ethnic mobilization are readily visible in neighboring Rwanda? Knowing that ethnic mobilization will likely precipitate attacks and counterattacks, why do they foment fear and hatred anyway? The answer lies, in part, in the incentive structure of the political game. When an ethnic entrepreneur perceives greater advantages for himself or his group from aggression, he is less likely to accept a second-preference solution such as power sharing. Steven Burg writes concerning the outbreak of civil war in Bosnia in 1992:

> Of all the ethnic leaderships one can think of, the Muslim nationalists in control of the Party of Democratic Action probably had more reason to fear violence than most. Yet, despite the obvious threat of violence, and of tremendous cost to their own community, they proceeded to override Serb concerns and to opt for independence rather than some form of association with the rest of the former Yugoslavia (mainly Serbia). It is easy to reconstruct their logic—better dead than Serb. . . . Ethnic leaderships often do choose violence and war over peace when they think their own political power (a cynical interpretation) or cultural survival of their people (a noble interpretation) is at stake.[1]

Therefore, at least one key to unlocking ethnic conflict situations is to focus on the structure and operation of incentives in periods of rapid political change; such an analysis can lead the international community to recognize under what conditions the promotion of power sharing is likely to bear fruit in terms of stabilizing intergroup relations. Burundi's fragile and troubled power-sharing pact, reached in the throes of crisis after the assassination of President Ntaryamira in April 1994 and known as the Convention of Government, is under strain as a result of the radicalization of the political landscape in that country, the fragmentation of the political field, and constant outbidding of moderates.[2] Yet for Burundi it may be too late for power sharing. There is wide agreement among scholars that early recognition and amelioration of intergroup tensions in the evolution of ethnic conflicts is better than late action; Horowitz, for example, contrasts the early efforts of Malaysian political leaders to defuse and manage tensions to the late efforts of Sri Lankans (1991:111–121).

Transitional Moments and Peace Processes

Moments of danger and opportunity arise when political systems are in flux. The events that prompt transitional politics may be external, such as the demise of an imperial power such as the Soviet Union and the end of the Cold War, or internal, when intergroup relations have reached a stalemate and parties see clear advantages in reorganizing their relationships. In both instances, transitions involve reconstituting the basic rules of the political game.

In the international sphere, for example, changes in the international game in the early 1990s led to new states and the belief by aggrieved ethnic groups that the moment was ripe for pressing claims for secession. In the domestic sphere, transitional periods, usually cast in terms of "democratization processes," clearly are moments of hope and peril. Transitions offer hope because the opportunity for institutionalizing peace exists; intergroup relations and rules of the political game are in flux, and parties may adopt conflict-regulating practices.

But such moments are equally perilous, for as an interregnum begins, incentives for ethnic mobilization and aggression may be stronger than those that lead to moderation (de Nevers 1993; Horowitz 1993). The absence of clearly defined rules of the game means a vacuum exists in which politics is confusing and its outcomes are deeply uncertain. Expectations, fears, and aspirations are rife. Renee de Nevers (1993) identifies seven factors that influence whether violent ethnic conflict will emerge in the course of a transition to democracy: (1) the speed at which ethnic issues are identified, (2) the level of ethnic tensions at the onset of a transition, (3) the size and power of groups, (4) the ethnic composition of the ancien régime and opposition, (5) the external relations of groups and states, (6) the composition of the military, and (7) the role of political leadership.

Yet in other instances, particularly those in which the Cold War had fueled or frozen enmities, political leaders have used transitional moments to de-escalate conflicts through extended peace processes. Global transitions such as the end of the Cold War can help precipitate ripe moments, in which parties have reached a mutually hurting stalemate and precipitating events have led political leaders to embrace a negotiated solution as a better alternative than continued violence. In such instances a key ingredient of success has been a sustained process of talks, characterized by the step-by-step adoption of pacts. Pacts are mutual security agreements in which parties forswear the use of violence to achieve their aims in exchange for protection under agreed-upon rules of the political game (O'Donnell, Schmitter, and Whitehead 1986, pt. IV:37–39).

Instances of parties moving toward more productive conflict management arrangements through negotiation include, for example, South Africa, Mozambique, Cambodia, El Salvador, Nicaragua, Namibia, and, more recently, Angola (some of these are ethnic conflicts, and others are not). In other instances, a nascent process of pact making has begun but is not yet complete, such as Northern Ireland and the Israel-Palestine track of the Middle East peace process. These cases conform to theories about the effects of a relative balance of power, namely, that relative symmetry in power relationships—for example, between an insurgent group and a government—and high levels of interdependency among groups account for the emergence of power-sharing practices (Du Toit 1989b). That is, insurgents are unable to defeat governments, but governments are unable to defeat insurgencies. So they opt for negotiated pacts.

This conclusion jibes with Terry Lynn Karl's findings that in Latin America consociational or corporatist outcomes emerged from pacted transitions to democracy (1990). Equally, where transitions (especially civil wars) end with one party clearly dominant, as in military victories, power sharing is an unlikely outcome. Many suggest that such unilateral victories are actually more stable than negotiated outcomes when stability is defined as the absence of renewed fighting (Pillar 1983; Wagner 1993).

In instances where negotiation processes achieve stable outcomes, political leaders perceive "exit options" from a peace process to be costly and disadvantageous. Political leaders who opt for peace find that, just as they were once trapped in a cycle of conflict, now the structure of incentives works to trap them in the politics of moderation. It is no surprise then, that leaders such as de Klerk and Mandela were perceived as being trapped in an "arranged marriage." Once a process of intergroup moderation begins, it can develop a certain momentum or inertia in which parties are locked into a pattern of cooperation because abandoning a negotiation process will leave them vulnerable to outbidders who opposed accommodation with ethnic enemies. For example, it is widely speculated that neither Israeli prime minister Rabin (or his successor, Shimon Peres) nor Palestine Liberation Organization chairman Yasir Arafat could have politically survived a collapse of the Middle East peace process, for it would prove their respective rejectionist foes correct.

Equally instructive, however, are those instances in which high levels of political violence have produced a mutually hurting stalemate but have *not* precipitated a meaningful negotiation process (such as in Kashmir or Algeria). These instances raise questions about the factors that propel processes of ethnic conflict management or the factors that lead parties to begin and sustain negotiations. Nordlinger and others are right to focus on elite attitudes in terms of necessary conditions for the onset of peace processes in times of transitions. Political leaders are often in the best position to recognize the costs of conflict and embrace a negotiation process that leads to the adoption of conflict-regulating practices. But the structure of incentives must be right for a process to begin and to be sustained, as Burg's analysis of the Bosnian Muslim leadership's calculus shows.

A critical element missing in previous analyses of the adoption of conflict-regulating practices is the relationship between elite attitudes and mass or popular beliefs. Nordlinger (1972:60) describes a "psycho-historical model of attitude formation" in deeply divided societies and insightfully argues that "politically secure leaders need to be relatively unconcerned with their own 'fall,' allowing them to engage in regulatory behavior with considerably less fear of weakening their positions" (1972:65). Clearly, political leaders in both India and Pakistan today, for example, feel too electorally weak to negotiate resolution of the Kashmir dispute, even if they were so inclined.

Recent experience confirms the Nordlinger thesis about the limited ability of political leaders to embrace intergroup moderation. Elite predominance may be a necessary condition for the onset of a peace process, but it is certainly not sufficient. If Nordlinger is correct that "successful or unsuccessful regulation will be largely dependent upon the purposeful behavior of political elites" (1972:4), and given the tendency of ethnic entrepreneurs to mobilize for personal gain, the question is, Why do political elites moderate, and to what end? Whereas thinkers such as Nordlinger have argued that elites need to control their constituencies, a more useful approach is to consider the issue in terms of elite abilities to persuade followers of the benefits of peaceful intergroup relations and to demobilize them when the moment of peace arrives. In short, deference is a matter not of stagnant authority but of mobilization and demobilization of constituencies and a constant exchange of communication between politicians and their publics.

For example, F. W. de Klerk was slightly more successful in persuading recalcitrant whites in South Africa to back the negotiation process than former Israeli prime minister Yitzhak Rabin was in maintaining a fragile governing coalition in support of the Oslo Declaration of Principles to make peace with Palestinians. Similarly, Sri Lankan prime minister Chandrika Kumaratunga won the presidency on a peace platform for the first time in her country's history, a message that resonated with a war-weary public across ethnic lines (Human Rights Watch 1995:95–96). Renewed violence, however, has ended a tentative cease-fire, and the enmities in Sri Lanka appear as intractable as ever. The extent to which political leaders can demobilize constituencies is a critical and often overlooked aspect of conflict management. Theories of ethnic conflict are much better at explaining ethnic group mobilization than demobilization.

Equally instructive are those situations in which political leaders have been unsuccessful in demobilizing ethnic constituencies in support of peace initiatives. In Rwanda, for example, after the genocidal carnage of April 1994 referred to above, leaders of the militarily victorious Tutsi-led Rwanda Patriotic Front (RPF) publicly committed themselves to policies of national reconciliation: the RPF prime minister appointed moderate Hutus to the cabinet and announced efforts to promote reconciliation in educational materials and tone down public rhetoric about the Hutu-Tutsi strife. Regrettably, the message of national reconciliation has not filtered down to the mobilized populace or to mid-level elites such as those in the military. The UN Secretary-General's former special representative in Rwanda, Shaharyar Khan, said in the wake of an estimated 2,000 deaths in an incident at the Kibeho refugee camp in late April 1995, "the public statements [on reconciliation] this government makes must be implemented down the line. . . . The promises, the commitments, must be carried out. Right now the message is not filtering through."[3]

Findings from South Africa (Sisk 1993b) and Northern Ireland (Duffy and Frensley 1989) suggest that the elite-mass dichotomy is too simplified and that pivotal players in peace processes are mobilized mid-level elites—that is, local, regional, or party and military or paramilitary functionaries whose immediate interests may be most threatened by a relaxation of intergroup tensions. An important variable in the sustainability of peace processes is the unity and coherence of parties to the conflict, including not only insurgent groups, governments, and political parties, but also those elements of civil society that are likely to be divided ethnically, such as business and trade unions.

Increasingly, international participants in ethnic conflict management processes are focusing simultaneously on bottom-up efforts (usually through activities of nongovernmental organizations) and top-down, or diplomatic, efforts. Perhaps an important missing link is the middle range of local- and regional-level group leaders whose direct interests—power and control—are at stake. For example, even the warlords in Somalia have their cadre of organized and agitated lieutenants to manage. Similarly, in Mozambique, winning RENAMO's (Mozambiquan National Resistance) acquiescence to a peace process involved side payments to its top political leaders and to its foot soldiers through demobilization programs. Successful policies aimed at peaceful management of ethnic conflicts must be targeted at multiple levels of society, more or less simultaneously.

When peace processes are initiated in deeply divided societies, their success depends not only on *broadening* the moderate political center—persuading rejectionist parties to participate in negotiations and in the new institutions that flow from them—but also on *deepening* moderation in society. How broad and sustainable is the political center? That is, does consensus depend on a small handful of political leaders, or does a broader spectrum of viewpoints embrace the peace process? How deep are feelings of ethnic enmities? That is, does the populace respond to the appeal of outbidders, undermining moderate political leaders as they seek to limit strife?

A final point regarding the process of introducing more peaceful intergroup relations is that peace processes do not end ethnic tensions but, rather, transform them. The onset of reconciliation talks entails both the adoption of cooperative strategies and the likelihood of continued conflict. In many instances the underlying causes of conflict persist even as political leaders assemble at a negotiating table to devise practices to manage them. This dialectic of cooperation and conflict leaves moderate elites exceptionally vulnerable to intragroup politics of outbidding and hostage—particularly in multipolar ethnic conflicts—to the attempts by spoilers (rejectionists) to derail negotiations. Thus, in virtually every conflict, accommodative pursuits are limited by the reality of achieving only limited or sufficient consensus on the new rules of the political game.[4]

The survivability of moderates in situations of deep ethnic enmity depends much on the international community's role in buttressing attempts to reach and sustain mutual security pacts and to transform initial pacts such as cease-fires into viable, long-term, democratic conflict-regulating practices, usually embodied in new constitutions. Horowitz writes that the goal of such "grand settlements" is to "find a minimal basis for living together" (1985:583). Critical in virtually every conflict management process is the fact that the implementation stage is as important as, if not more important than, either the onset of negotiations or the clinching of a settlement. Rothchild writes, "Ethnic bargaining can be the origin of civility, but the implementation process is something that the actors can only achieve through a continuance of negotiations. Peacemaking is not achieved through a single negotiation, but through an extended process of negotiations" (1995:69).

6

International Intervention and Power Sharing

Although the international community has been persuasive and even coercive in attempts to coax leaders of conflicting ethnic groups into power-sharing arrangements as a means of preventing or escaping violent conflict, it is ultimately up to the parties themselves to agree to accept a form of democratic decision making that is inevitably something less than their stronger preference for complete control of their group's destiny. Many thoughtful analysts of the politics of divided societies are appropriately pessimistic about the ability of the international community to significantly affect the outcomes of ethnic conflicts. Donald Horowitz writes, "What stands out is just how ineffective the international community has been in imposing a modicum of civility on even those small states one might have thought it was in a position to coerce: Rwanda, Burundi, Somalia, Bosnia, etc. Actually, when states themselves have taken the initiative, they have done better—which suggests that these domestic problems are best handled domestically, although they are rarely handled well at all."[1]

Power sharing usually flows out of a history of violent conflict or as an attempt to preempt the degeneration of intergroup relations into violence. In many contemporary instances, the international community—usually but not always through the United Nations— has intervened in civil wars and advocated power-sharing practices as part of the political component of broader efforts to manage the

many facets of the complex emergencies spawned by these conflicts.[2] Power-sharing outcomes, it will be seen, are the result of
many of these interventions.

For example, in Liberia a coalition of international mediators
(including the United Nations, the Organization of African Unity,
the West African regional organization ECOWAS [Economic
Community of West African States], and U.S. diplomats) brokered a
pact in August 1995 among the three major armed factions that
establishes a transitional Council of State inclusive of all three major
armed factions. The civil war in Liberia has been one of the world's
most costly recent ethnic conflicts—150,000 people lost their lives,
and more than half of the country's 2.6 million people are displaced.
The agreement on power sharing is a critical step in the effort to
restore peace in Liberia, although much depends on its implementation and on the prospects for stability as this grand coalition seeks
to manage the difficult tasks of creating a new political system (including holding elections in 1996), reconstructing a war-torn economy,
demobilizing and reintegrating militias, and resettling returning
refugees and displaced persons. After five years of war and twice as
many failed agreements, it appears that international intervention in
Liberia has finally arrived at an outcome acceptable to all the parties
to that brutal conflict.

Yet rarely are the models, options, and plans formulated by international mediators in the course of peace processes informed by a
coherent analysis of the basic approaches to power sharing and the
principal institutions and practices that foster ethnic conflict management outlined in the preceding chapters. Instead, the approach is usually ad hoc, in which diplomats and analysts seek to craft appropriate
solutions given the expected willingness of the parties to accept alternative outcomes, or in some instances (such as Angola, described
below) after the parties attempted majoritarian democracy and failed,
precipitating a new round of costly violence. What is immediately
feasible and minimally acceptable to the parties often comes before
what is desirable in terms of conflict management over the long term.

This chapter considers ways in which the international community, in the course of efforts to prevent simmering conflicts from

escalating or to mediate settlements in ongoing civil wars, can more systematically encourage the adoption of conflict-mitigating mechanisms in deeply divided societies in a manner better informed by scholarly analysis of power-sharing practices and with a keener awareness of the pitfalls and risks associated with them.[3]

Are Existing Borders Sacrosanct?

When challenged by severe ethnic conflicts, decision makers in the international community must first ask a prior, fundamental question: Is maintaining the cohesion and territorial integrity of a given state a desirable, feasible outcome? Can Sudan's warring groups ever coexist peacefully? Should Rwanda and Burundi be bifurcated into Tutsi and Hutu states? Should the international community recognize a de facto independent Nagorno-Karabakh? What would happen if members of the international community recognized an independent Chechnya? While secessionist tendencies are created by domestic conditions, whether they succeed or fail is ultimately up to the international community, which can choose to recognize a group's right to territorial sovereignty and self-determination or to deny recognition.

The question of boundary change is a highly unsettled issue in international law and practice. Most boundary changes in the post–World War II era were the result of decolonization (including the partition of India and Pakistan), and some recent boundary changes (such as Eritrea and Namibia) are essentially the last instances of the postwar decolonization. When faced with essentially ethnic conflicts in which groups seek self-determination through secession, with few exceptions (the creation of Bangladesh, for example) the international community has an institutional tendency to do nothing or very little, invoking the principle of noninterference and implicitly denying group self-determination claims; to focus on international norms of human rights and the principles of democracy, but not to stress self-determination as a principle; or to invoke the right of self-determination but rule out secession, insisting that groups go on living together.

Only in more recent years, with particular reference to the collapse of the former Soviet Union, the dissolution of a federated Yugoslavia, and the bifurcation of the former Czechoslovakia, has the international community endorsed the creation of new states outside of the decolonization framework. In Czechoslovakia it was primarily the Slovaks who sought to exit a shared state, and the outcome in Slovakia has not been democratic. The dissolution of the former Yugoslavia was a watershed in this regard. At the European Union's 1992 Conference on the Former Yugoslavia, the possibility of maintaining Yugoslavia's territorial integrity was not even proposed by the European Union as an option.

The velvet divorce in Czechoslovakia aside, an ethnic group's claims for self-determination are usually indicative of severe human rights violations, and the conflict is often in a late stage. Secession *is* a solution of last resort, and many groups today do not perceive coexistence with their opponents as acceptable. The international community is often rightly concerned primarily with the *process* of change, that is, whether change is peaceful or violent. But it is also involved in shaping the outcome, that is, the terms of settlement. International insistence on maintaining the territorial integrity of Bosnia and Herzegovina has been a critical factor in shaping the outcome of that conflict.

If political divorce is relatively peaceful—or "velvet," as in the former Czechoslovakia—there is no sound reason to insist on maintaining a state's boundaries as long as the outcome is sustainable, mutually acceptable to the parties, and expected to be internally democratic. That may well be the case with Canada's Quebec. Rather than to simply eschew secession, the task is to develop clear guidelines on when and under what circumstances secessionist efforts will be supported by the international community and when they will be opposed. Are a sovereign state and self-determination the prize of victory in a violent struggle (as in Eritrea) or of a negotiated settlement (as in Czechoslovakia)? Is at least one party willing to fight to the bitter end for a state's survival in its current form?

The international community usually responds to contemporary ethnic conflicts by emphasizing that states and insurgent groups must adhere to international norms of human rights, democracy, and, increasingly, protection of minority rights *within* existing states. UN Secretary-General Boutros Boutros-Ghali, in the 1995 "Supplement to the Agenda for Peace," refers to the challenge of intrastate wars, "often of a religious or ethnic character," and asserts that "international intervention must extend beyond military and humanitarian tasks and must include the promotion of national reconciliation and the re-establishment of effective government, [including] the design and supervision of constitutional, judicial, and electoral reforms."[4]

When the international community deems a state viable, but parties to ethnic conflicts cannot come to terms on the criteria for the establishment of their political system, intervention by the international community plays a critical role. As Boutros-Ghali wrote, "the time of absolute and exclusive sovereignty . . . has passed" (1992:9). Insisting on a common state, and a democratic one at that, begs a critical question. As a preeminent theorist of democracy, Robert Dahl, writes (1989:207), "When does a collection of persons constitute an entity—'a people'—entitled to govern itself democratically?" As Pierre du Toit notes, "when domestic adversaries cannot agree on the [viability and scope of their state], only the international community remains to express judgement. And on the basis of what norms, rules, and guidelines?"[5]

Dahl provides the following seven guidelines (1989:207–209), applicable to the international community's decisions about the feasibility of existing states, which must all be satisfied for a democratic political state to be viable. First, the domain and the scope of the unit must be clearly identified, or "bounded"; the more indeterminate the domain and scope, the greater the likelihood of jurisdictional disputes or civil wars. Second, there must be agreement on the scope of political autonomy, avoiding the twin dangers of granting autonomy when it is not wanted and denying it when it is demanded. Third, the people must strongly desire to govern themselves according to the democratic process: "The claim of a group to political autonomy is less justifiable the more likely it is that their new government will not respect the democratic process. The right to self-determination entails no right to form an oppressive government," he writes. Fourth, the establishment of a new unit of politics cannot inflict serious harm, neither to its own members nor to others outside its boundaries. Fifth, a claim to self-determination cannot be advanced by persons whose interests are not directly affected by that claim. Sixth, one set of boundaries is better than many if it provides for greater opportunities for the exercise of personal freedoms. Seventh, "measured by all relevant criteria, the gains must outweigh the costs."

Dahl concludes that "in the real world, then, answers to the question of what constitutes a people for democratic purposes are far more likely to come from political action and conflict, which will often be accompanied by violence and coercion, than from reasoned inferences on democratic principles and action (1989:209)." This statement is certainly borne out by experience. When existing states are deemed viable and desirable by the international community, a subsequent question arises: How can the international community work toward the introduction of conflict-mitigating practices?

International Mediation

If the principal aim of international intervention in internal conflicts is to promote, as Boutros-Ghali asserts, "the creation of structures for the institutionalization of peace,"[6] policymakers should direct their attention to the two levels of incentive structures to which parties in conflict may respond. The first and most critical incentives on which to focus are those at the level of states, where the rules of the game may effectively reward interethnic toleration, inclusivity, and a respect for rights. Does the political system reward ethnic exclusion, chauvinism, and elite excitation of popular intolerance? Transitional moments and protracted peace processes provide opportunities, or entry points, for international intervention to help structure political systems—democratic ones, ideally—that can ameliorate ethnic conflict.

The second level is the international system, where international norms and rules may either encourage or discourage fissiparous tendencies and lead parties to believe either that violent attempts to gain self-determination will be successful or that violent oppression of disadvantaged groups' rights will be ignored or go unsanctioned. For example, the post–Cold War international system may contain incentives for subnational groups to press secessionist aims; recognition of the constituent parts of the former Yugoslavia serves as a "demonstration effect" that partition of existing states is a distinct possibility. Revision of existing norms and the development of new norms by international organizations is a critical aspect of appropriately structuring incentives to promote intergroup cooperation. The reformulation of international norms on minority rights is discussed more fully in this section below.

What is lacking in the current discourse on the promotion of democracy as a response to ethnic conflict is the realization that the international community need not always advocate simple forms of majoritarian democracy—usually manifested in terms of encouraging and even coercing parties into early elections as the culminating event of a peace process.[7] Charles Maynes, for example, decries a cultural bias in U.S. policy that places a premium on individual rights, majoritarian elections, and federalism (1993). At times, he suggests, it is equally appropriate to encourage the adoption of power-sharing democracy by means of some of the conflict-regulating approaches and practices sketched in chapters 3 and 4.

The promotion of power-sharing practices can, under appropriate circumstances, be a critical aspect of the international response to complex emergencies emanating from ethnic conflicts. It should be used in tandem with other instruments of diplomacy: military and economic sanctions, diplomatic and economic inducements, mediation, facilitation, "good offices," electoral assistance, and in the most extreme cases—such as Cambodia and Mozambique—international administration of the peace process. Although normally considered in terms of peace building, the promotion of conflict-mitigating practices can equally be introduced as a matter of preventive diplomacy before a conflict deepens into intractable violence.

The international community has an interest in the nature of outcomes to ethnic conflicts. When outcomes may occur that reward aggression or violate international norms of fairness, when the consequences of an outcome harm neighbors or other states, or when a precedent set for the international system is unacceptable, the international community has a clear interest not only in the peaceful resolution of disputes but also in the terms that resolve them. Tools of international diplomacy, including force, can be applied to get parties to the table or keep them there, where they may well arrive at power-sharing arrangements. NATO air strikes against the Bosnian Serbs have clearly influenced the process by which a confederal power-sharing arrangement was reached in the Bosnian war in the November 1995 Dayton Accords. This solution, as mentioned briefly in chapter 3, is interesting precisely because it straddles the fence between partition and power sharing, including both shared institutions (a rotating presidency and a parliament with built-in mutual vetoes) and separate territorial entities with special ties to other states.

Intervention to promote power sharing is an act of mediation, involving helping parties analyze the nature of their conflicts, introducing formulas and options, wielding sticks and offering carrots to induce parties to accept solutions believed to be appropriate (or simply to encourage them to remain within the negotiation process), exercising power to create conditions conducive to a settlement, helping implement agreements, and even enforcing them (Bercovitch 1989, 1992; Touval and Zartman 1985). The timing of intervention strategies is likewise important, suggesting that intervention should be timed to build on, or to produce, critical turning points in relations that lead parties from an adversarial stance to a collaborative problem-solving posture.[8] It is important to note that mediators invariably bring their own interests to the table, if only an interest in moving the parties toward a negotiated settlement. The bias of mediators is to get an agreement. In working with ethnic conflicts, however, this is a potential problem. Horowitz rightly notes that "mediators have a process bias that keeps them from focusing on good institutional arrangements, in favor of 'getting to yes,' any yes."[9] This process bias can lead to very unfortunate outcomes, such as in the 1992 election in Angola.

In efforts to avoid future ethnic conflicts and end current ones, the international community will increasingly play a critical role in ensuring that parties negotiate mutually beneficial outcomes, that in the course of redesigning the rules of the political game minorities are treated fairly, and that groups can feel sufficiently secure to concede to the inevitable uncertainty of democratic elections. Recent experience shows that intervention in civil wars is fraught with difficulties inherent in the nature of contemporary ethnic conflicts (Stedman 1995)—incoherent parties, lack of leverage to affect the perceptions and actions of insurgent groups and their leaders, and parties' insincere commitment to peace.

The international community can at least provide disputants with information and analysis based on the experiences of other states to help them craft more effective political structures. Information counts. A good example is the interactive video debate sponsored by the United States Information Agency on appropriate electoral systems for postapartheid South Africa (featuring professors Lijphart and Horowitz together with top South African constitutional thinkers) in September 1990, just as the parties were beginning to develop their positions in anticipation of constitutional talks. This debate, among the other suggestions offered for South Africa by power-sharing analysts, clearly informed and improved the debate about effective conflict-regulating practices for that deeply divided society.[10]

More recently, parliamentary leaders from Burundi have been taken on fact-finding trips to South Africa, and South Africans have gone to Burundi, to help discover lessons from the transition from apartheid that may be applicable to ameliorating tensions between Tutsis and Hutus. Awareness of what has and has not worked to ameliorate ethnic conflicts in other states can help disputants think through the consequences of their choices. Further, states such as South Africa that have experienced some success in reorienting their intergroup relations away from violent conflict clearly have a special role to play in international intervention elsewhere, bringing not only leverage but knowledge, experience, and a great deal of understanding as well.

In some instances, intervention has been indirect, shepherding a negotiation process but allowing the parties to arrive at their own settlement terms. In others, intervention has been more intrusive, involving support for disadvantaged parties to affect the balance of power in efforts to produce stable outcomes, as in Bosnia. Indeed, promoting power sharing is perhaps the most intrusive aspect of international intervention; Elazar correctly asserts that constitutional design is the "pre-eminently political act" (1985). Recent experience in Rwanda and Somalia, for example, highlights that the peace-building phase of intervention, of which power sharing may be an integral part, is the most difficult to achieve.

An important aspect of current mediation efforts in instances of deep ethnic conflicts is that mediation is rarely conducted by a single individual, state, or even international organization such as the United Nations (Touval 1994). The more common situation is a coalition of mediators, sometimes working in concert with close coordination of goals and strategies—as in Mozambique (Hume 1994)—and sometimes pulling in opposite directions (as in Sudan[11]). Further, mediation efforts may be less intrusive or even indirect, such as bestowing the Nobel Peace Prize on leaders such as South African peacemakers F. W. de Klerk and Nelson Mandela or Yitzhak Rabin and Yasir Arafat in order to bolster their standing internationally and among their own publics. Or mediation may be direct and highly intrusive, such as offering specific plans and terms for a settlement.

There is widespread belief that in the wake of failed or faltering international interventions to reconstitute peaceful politics in Somalia and Bosnia, the international community must derive other options and approaches to intervention in ethnic conflicts. At least one option is the early promotion of power sharing. The international community can help parties think through the consequences of their choices for creating appropriate democratic institutions in deeply divided societies in a manner that does not lead immediately to majoritarian practices—practices that simply reconstitute the zero-sum game of the battlefield into a zero-sum game for a presidency or for control of parliament.

Formulas and Options

External intervention moves beyond facilitation to mediation when the external party seeks to influence the outcome of negotiations, either by influencing the balance of power or by offering formulas and options for a settlement of the conflict (Touval and Zartman 1985). In offering formulas for settlement to parties, mediators can increase the information available to negotiators and may provide face-saving exits from firmly entrenched positions. Effective mediators must have a keen sense of the parties' perceptions of each other and the mediator, an awareness of which demands are negotiable, and a strategic sense of time.

Although there are many instances of option-mongering to establish power sharing in deeply divided societies, it is instructive to analyze several recent formulas and their impact on the parties in conflict. Again, the conflict in Bosnia is instructive. In October 1992, the United Nations and European Union mediators Cyrus Vance and Lord David Owen introduced a "Framework for a New Constitution" that would have established seven to ten "administratively and economically viable" provinces within a confederal framework.[12] The Vance-Owen plan is premised on the belief that Bosnia's population is "inextricably intermingled. Thus, there appears to be no viable way to create three territorially distinct states based on ethnic or confessional principles." Given this belief, and because a highly centralized state was opposed by at least two of the three major parties to the conflict, devolution and power sharing appeared to be a logical response. The Vance-Owen plan envisaged the following:

- Seven to ten provinces, most of which would include ethnic minorities, but whose names would not reflect ethnic identities.
- No overt recognition of groups, but acknowledgment that the political process is likely to be dominated by group identity; therefore certain posts or functions would be allocated to achieve proportional communal representation and conscious protection of minorities.

- A weak, almost minimalist, central government with powers over defense, foreign affairs, international commitments, and issues related to common citizenship.
- A national legislature elected on the basis of strict proportionality, and an upper house or senate drawn from provincial governments, also on the basis of proportionality.
- A presidency comprising as many individuals as there are provinces, with a president that would ideally be a neutral figure who commands respect from all of the major groups; a prime minister's position would be based on group rotation and balance.
- Integrated civil and military services, reflective of relative group strength and based on the principle of nondiscrimination in recruitment, promotion, and supervision.
- Creation of special judicial processes, for example, a human rights court, ombudsmen for group rights, and special minority protections based on UN resolutions and other international legal instruments.

The Vance-Owen plan—based on principles of balance, rotation, integration, and nondiscrimination—is perhaps the most detailed power-sharing plan to be offered by a mediator in a contemporary conflict situation and will likely continue to serve as a model even though it was not adopted by the parties to the conflict. It included the promotion of both consociational and integrative mechanisms in the same package.

The failure of the parties to accept the Vance-Owen plan is indicative of situations in which mediators offer formulas without sufficient leverage. The Bosnian Serbs refused to give up hope for a "Greater Serbia," and some observers allege that the plan drove a wedge between the Croats and the Muslims. John Chipman writes concerning the plan: "The international community can do many things in ethnic conflict management, but one thing it cannot do is force an oath of fealty to a state when many of the inhabitants believe it is artificial. Without that promise, structural agreements for the state itself are without foundation" (1993:256).

When conflict lines seem to run especially deep, as in the former Yugoslavia, radical partition or dividing territory may be the only possible solution for peace, notwithstanding the normative implications of ratifying territorial gains made through aggression.[13] For this reason the essentially confederal plan recently agreed to by the leadership of the three communities there maintains the territorial integrity of the state. The international community's adherence to norms and principles—outcomes over process—in the Bosnian war points out a key dilemma in international mediation. As Saadia Touval writes, "Conceivably, insistence of respect for international norms, insistence that members of different nationalities must live together side by side in peace, and that ethnic partition will violate this principle, may have contributed to extending the war with its terrible cost of human suffering" (1995).

The inability to achieve a more integrative power-sharing solution in Bosnia contains many lessons, but clearly one of them is the limitation of mediation in ethnic conflicts. Stedman succinctly outlines the dilemma of a mediator under such conditions: "When superiors demand a just peace, and one is not possible because of the military power of one side, then a mediator should demand from his or her superiors a decision on whether to compromise one's morality to achieve peace, engage in peace-enforcement, or walk away from the conflict" (1995:54).

When power sharing fails, partition short of state dissolution remains an option notwithstanding the normative and practical difficulties of this outcome. In a (now clearly unsuccessful) attempt to stave off a recurrence of the war in Croatia in early 1995, a coalition of mediators, including the U.S. and Russian ambassadors to Zagreb along with two officials of the International Conference on the Former Yugoslavia, proffered a power-sharing plan that relied heavily on confederal territorial divisions of power.[14] The plan, known at the time as the Z-4 plan, would have provided nearly complete self-government to the Croatian Serbs in those areas captured by them in the 1991 war. A Western diplomat pointed out, "This plan offers the Serbs everything they can possibly achieve in the real world. . . . They will never have their own state in Croatia and there will never be a greater Serbia. But to convince them of this is virtually impossible."[15] Croatia's government, too, rejected the plan, arguing that the autonomy proposals went too far in giving Croatian Serbs the trappings of a modern state. Efforts to induce the parties to accept the plan, which was based on the diplomats' best effort at a mutually acceptable solution, failed with renewed fighting in May 1995. By August 1995, Croatia essentially eradicated the problem of Krajina in a military campaign by driving the Serb minority into Bosnia.

Other examples of mediator formulas to end a conflict through some variant of power sharing abound and are illustrative of the range of options available in crafting conflict-appropriate solutions.

- In August 1992 UN Secretary-General Boutros Boutros-Ghali proffered a "Set of Ideas" for Cyprus, which degenerated into a civil war in 1963 in part over differences of interpretation of the power-sharing clauses of the postindependence constitution. In the latest of myriad attempts by the world body to mediate the conflict, Boutros-Ghali touted the establishment of a unified but "bi-zonal, bi-federal" state, replete with proportional communal representation, special majorities, group rights, territorial adjustments, and transitional arrangements.[16]

- For the conflict over Nagorno-Karabakh, former Organization of Security and Cooperation in Europe (OSCE) mediator John Maresca put forward a plan in September 1994 that, while essentially an autonomy arrangement for the enclave, included proportional representation and minority group rights for Armenians in Azerbaijan and Azeris in Nagorno-Karabakh legislatures, respectively.[17]

- The recently released joint Anglo-Irish "Framework Document" for settlement of the Northern Ireland dispute also contains some power-sharing elements, particularly the proposed new Northern Ireland ninety-seat assembly in which five members from each of the present parliamentary constituencies are elected on the basis of proportional representation and decisions within the assembly are taken by weighted voting on "contentious issues."[18] Although the United Kingdom and

Ireland are in many ways both disputants and mediators, the document will serve as a basis for further talks and wide public debate on the territory's future dispensation.

As the foregoing discussion suggests, the options and formulas for power sharing vary widely on a case-by-case basis. When considering introducing a formula or a more specific option for the mitigation of an ethnic conflict, the international community should be better aware of the wide range of options that have, at least in some instances, resulted in successful conflict management practices. Clearly, which basic approach, consociational or integrative, and which mix of conflict-regulating practices may be appropriate in a given situation cannot be determined in advance. Nor can the issue of whether the parties are sufficiently flexible to accept a mediator's package at any given time. What the parties may accept at one moment may well be radically different from what they are willing to accept at another, especially after armed encounters change the structure of relations on the ground.

Inducements

In addition to offering formulas and options, mediators may seek to influence parties by employing incentives and disincentives—carrots and sticks—to encourage parties to end violence and begin to negotiate, to lead them to agreement, or to affect the terms of a settlement. In many recent instances, mediators have employed the traditional diplomatic instruments to induce parties to adopt conflict-regulating practices in attempts to ameliorate ethnic conflicts. The challenges to policymakers is to determine not only the right formula but also the mix of inducements that will lead parties to adopt an agreement that is legitimate, stable, and acceptable to the international community. Inducements, it should be readily noted, are but an aid to a mediator whose principal resources are knowledge, persuasion, and standing with the parties. Inducements can be tangible, such as the imposition of sanctions, military force or the threat of force, offers of guarantees, or side payments to parties; or intangible, such as bestowing legitimacy by engaging a particular disputant in talks.

Finally, before inducements can be effective, a mediator must have a prior understanding of what outcomes are acceptable to the parties, the mediator, and the international community. Mediators bring their own interests to the table and are generally more successful when they limit their goals to a specific and achievable objective, taking into account what Alexander George has termed the "asymmetry of motivation" (1993b:13). Some parties are more doggedly motivated to adhere to or advance their positions because the depth of their commitment is comparatively strong. In matters of ethnic conflict, the vital interests—survival—of groups are usually at stake.

A power-sharing pact is by its nature a complex objective to achieve. Waterman (1993:287) argues that inducements to hasten or delay a settlement of a civil war are more effective than those that seek to affect the shape of the settlement. Mediators are more likely to succeed in shaping the settlement when they are working on a specific conflict than when they are promoting ethnic conflict management more broadly. Jenonne Walker (1993) differentiates between "hard" mediation in ethnic conflicts—that is, concentrated efforts by individual eminent persons, states, or international organizations to resolve a specific dispute—and "soft" mediation, or the broader question of "what outsiders can legitimately and usefully do to ease tensions among groups" through the creation of international norms and the structure of international institutions (1993:168). The dichotomy is useful, because in recent experience the international community has used both types of mediation to encourage parties to adopt power-sharing practices. An alternative and more precise set of terms is *operational mediation*, aimed at a specific circumstance, and *structural mediation*, aimed at the general behavior of states and ethnic groups.

A good example of operational mediation is the recent role of the international community in forging a power-sharing pact in Angola. International involvement in the events leading to power sharing in Angola also highlights the difficulties of mediator coordination and the vexing normative trade-offs that arise in intervention to end bitter internal conflicts. Angola's civil war, which has raged since independence in 1976, almost came to an end in 1991 when the parties agreed to a settlement (the Estoril Accords) and agreed to compete in a UN-monitored election in November 1992. The election event was fraught with crises, and the results of the voting—although declared free and fair by the UN monitors—was contested by the loser, UNITA (National Union for the Total Independence of Angola). The electoral system, especially for the directly elected president, was strictly majoritarian—a French-style plurality-plus-runoff system, which in effect guarantees a zero-sum game between the top two presidential candidates. Expecting to lose a subsequent runoff for the presidency after the incumbent president Jose dos Santos garnered 49 percent of the votes in the initial round of balloting, UNITA leader Jonas Savimbi demanded power sharing. Although the United Nations was not enthusiastic about the demand, given the first-round clear election outcome, the United States—a long-time Cold War patron of UNITA—backed Savimbi's claims but did not prevail. Rather than accept defeat, UNITA returned to the battlefield.

The war resumed until November 1994, when UN special envoy Bloudin Beye, backed by major global and regional powers, clinched a new settlement (the Lusaka Protocols) after protracted talks. The pact includes power-sharing features such as three reserved governorships for UNITA in areas it controls militarily, four minor cabinet positions, and a number of mayoral slots. Stedman (1995:44–46) notes that the 1992 U.S. decision to impose sanctions on its erstwhile client UNITA, along with many other levers of influence exerted by mediators, was critical in bringing UNITA to accept the terms of the agreement.[19] However, Stedman also laments the policy of promoting power sharing, seeing it as rewarding Savimbi's intransigence. In his view, power sharing as an outcome in Angola also sets a dangerous precedent for other disputants: belligerence can pay handsome dividends in the long run if a strong state or the international community will ultimately back demands for power sharing.[20] Unlike the earlier attempts to reach peace in Angola, the Lusaka agreement is likely to hold because of the implicit agreement to postpone new elections for some time to come, essentially delaying democratization in the pursuit of peace.

The Angolan case also highlights that international mediators have missed important opportunities to influence the course of conflicts. The choice for a French-style presidential system in the November 1992 election was unambiguously poor, almost ensuring that the leaders of the two principal armed factions would go head-to-head for the country's most powerful post, as they ultimately did. Why the mediators of the 1991 pact that led to the elections did not intrude and encourage the adoption of a different electoral system, or fail to back the pact if the parties insisted on a majoritarian system, remains a mystery. A different electoral system may not have ensured success in Angola, but it could have made success more likely.

In addition to long, hard, and complex *operational* mediation of the sort that occurred in Angola, *structural* mediation, such as the setting of international norms on minority rights, is quickly becoming an important lever of influence whereby the international community can encourage the adoption of conflict-regulating practices in multiethnic societies. The 1992 UN General Assembly resolution on rights of minorities (the "Minority Rights Resolution") declares that states are obliged to protect and encourage conditions that promote minority rights, defined in terms of individuals' rights to enjoy their cultures and languages, practice religion, and freely associate.[21] Norm setting has been taken a step further in European institutions, where security organizations such as the Council of Europe, the European Union, and OSCE have attached conditions for Eastern European states' membership in these institutions on equitable treatment of minorities, including several practices such as territorial and corporate autonomy and group rights. In international law and practice, clearer articulation of common standards to protect minority rights, along with measures designed to ensure compliance and arbitrate disputes (such as the Council of Europe's Court of Human Rights), are important steps forward in Europe. However, they rely principally on state compliance with international commitments. International norms are important but generally lack coherent, regularized enforcement procedures.

Increasingly, the international community should rely on linkages such as membership in, or access to, collective security or global trade regimes to help promote conflict-mitigating practices in multiethnic societies. The lure of membership in the emerging post–Cold War European security institutions (principally the NATO Partnership for Peace program and the Western European Union) and economic architecture, potentially full European Union membership, helps explain the March 1995 agreement between Hungary and Slovakia on the rights of the more than one-half million ethnic Hungarians in Slovakia.[22] A similar pact may be signed between Hungary and Romania, where 1.5 million Hungarians reside. As Steven Burg notes, however, "the problem up to now has been that none of these organizations, especially not the CE [Council of Europe] and the OSCE, have exercised any pressure on states and their leaders to conform before extending the privileges and status of membership." Thus, the leverage is still quite weak. After the Slovak government signed the March 1995 agreement, Burg adds, it sent "a unilateral note of understanding stipulating that the treaty did not mean that Slovakia had accepted Council of Europe obligations in this area."[23]

Incentives or conditions such as these mandated by European and transatlantic institutions, and the potential for isolation and sanction in the absence of such agreements, are potentially powerful tools to induce states—particularly in situations of majority domination—to embrace conflict-regulating practices such as the protection of group rights. Economic assistance policies as well as political pressures can be introduced with the aim of promoting the protection of minorities and improving the effect of public policies on ethnic relations. And pressures to introduce market economies, private property, and open media generate economic interests that help form convergences of interest across lines of ethnic enmity. Civil society organizations can emerge along lines of voluntary, not ascriptive, interests. With the Eastern European states in a very formative period in their political and economic development today, the opportunities for influencing the subsequent course of ethnic relations are particularly good.

The OSCE has been the most proactive international organization in recognizing collective rights as an element of international law and developing compliance mechanisms. The Concluding Document of the OSCE's 1991 Conference on National Minorities committed the signatory parties to establishing advisory and decision-making bodies in which minorities are represented, particularly on education, cultural, and religious issues; to establishing local autonomous administrative structures in territories where minorities reside; to embracing corporate federalism when minorities are not territorially concentrated; and to establishing permanent ethnically mixed interstate commissions when ethnic groups reside on different sides of an international frontier.[24]

The OSCE has also been the most innovative international organization in seeking to promote ethnic conflict management through preventive diplomacy. Its norms are enhanced through the work of new and innovative institutions such as the organization's High Commissioner on National Minorities in Europe (currently Max van der Stoel), which gives the organization a permanent mechanism for early warning of deteriorating ethnic relations and a rapid response instrument to help stave off escalation (Conflict Management Group 1993). The commissioner has already seen some success in preventive diplomacy interventions in Romania and Estonia since the office was established in 1992.

Innovative conditions and mechanisms for monitoring are important inducements, but they are usually directed at states, not at state subunits such as ethnic movements or militias. In dealing with nonstate disputants, the international community's options are more limited. How can the international community effectively engage the government of Chechnya (a constituent element of a sovereign state, the Russian Federation) to moderate its demands for secession? Although states and international organizations may be limited in their dealings with these entities by virtue of their charters or the principle of noninterference, functional bodies such as GATT or the World Trade Organization—whose membership rules are less restrictive than Article 4 of the UN Charter, which limits membership to states—are potentially promising levers of influence.

Membership or affiliation with these more flexible organizations can be a pragmatic way to impose conditions that may encourage parties to be more moderate. They can even have effects on nondemocratic states, such as China, or states that are at a very early and precarious stage of democratization, such as Russia.

More coercive options are also available, although arguably less effective, such as the imposition of sanctions on a state subentity (for example, Angola's UNITA). Bilateral and multilateral aid conditions for the equitable treatment of minorities through democratic practices remain a powerful tool; aid can be cut off when parties violate international norms (as in U.S. aid to Kenya), or it can be provided as a reward to parties who behave moderately (as in U.S. aid to Rwanda's fledgling national unity government).[25] When moderation on divisive ethnic themes yields tangible results—through increased development aid, for example—leaders willing to risk power-sharing practices may be better able to sustain themselves against the outbidding of extremists.

Finally, nontraditional diplomatic instruments may also be used to induce ethnic groups to adopt conflict-regulating practices. Effective "track two," or unofficial, diplomacy may help build a cadre of moderates and encourage creative problem solving, especially in prenegotiation situations (Saunders 1985). Nongovernmental organizations, such as the International Foundation for Electoral Systems or the Democratic and Republican international institutes in the United States, which provide election-related support, can also provide critical information to parties that may allow them to adopt practices that avoid zero-sum electoral competition. The establishment of the Electoral Assistance Division in the UN Department of Peacekeeping Operations is a positive step in this direction, although this unit can provide assistance only when a state requests it. Clearly, the regular and persistent investigative reports of nongovernmental human rights organizations have some effect on states to limit or curb ethnic enmities, essentially embarrassing regimes in the eyes of the world community.

In addition to improving existing mechanisms, developing new institutions aimed at influencing disputants in ethnic conflicts may be required. For example, U.S. Secretary of State Warren Christopher mooted a plan in 1993 to create an international tribunal to hear the grievances of ethnic minorities and to arbitrate (not mediate) disputes between ethnic groups and states or among groups themselves.[26]

Timing and Early Intervention

Even with the right formulas and a powerful mix of inducements, mediator interventions may fail without appropriate timing. Timing is critical in intervention strategies in two important respects: First, the conflict should be sufficiently ripe that a mediator formula or mediator actions will receive a favorable response from the parties in conflict. Second, the intervention should be timed at an appropriate juncture in the development of a conflict, for example, to prevent the widening or deepening escalation of a conflict, to clinch a settlement, or to check the reemergence of a conflict in the post-settlement implementation phase.

There is an emerging, albeit certainly not unanimous, consensus that early action and preventive diplomacy are better than late or no action to prevent conflict escalation. Väyrynen and Leatherman summarize the prevailing view well when they write that early intervention to forge a sustainable system of mediating intergroup conflicts can "control the vertical escalation of conflict (escalation in the use of violent means), and contain its horizontal spread (e.g., widening among more parties, or spill-over into new states, etc.)" (1995:3). In a comment specifically related to the promotion of democracy to manage ethnic conflicts, Larry Diamond and Marc Plattner suggest, "As the tragedy in the former Yugoslavia illustrates, once the dynamics of violent conflict takes over, hatred, fear, and vengeance—however 'modern'—may overwhelm rationality" (1994:xxii). Burg argues that the time to intervene in the former Yugoslavia "was in 1989 and 1990, when the competitive electoral process was being established. That was the moment when Horowitzian [proposals for integrative electoral systems, such as vote pooling] might have been established; but only if international actors make it clear to local leaders that 'recognition' was contingent on democratic outcomes."[27] Because integrative electoral system choices, which encourage vote pooling, place the onus of negotiation and compromise on local-level elites, they create pressures to pluralize, Burg adds.

Better appreciation of the timing of international intervention is essential if future opportunities to assist parties in adopting conflict-regulating practices are not to be missed. Elections illustrate how such opportunities are missed. It is widely appreciated that elections are a critical aspect of contemporary peace processes to manage conflict and introduce democracy, as Burg notes above. Elections can mitigate conflict by removing some of the uncertainty that is rife in a transitional process and being the culmination of a peace process (as in El Salvador or South Africa), or they can exacerbate conflict when they are crisis ridden. When elections have gone very wrong or have had disastrous consequences in highly conflictual societies (for example, Angola in November 1992, Algeria in December 1991, Burundi in June 1993) a rather simple majoritarian electoral system was at work, and the parties entered the contest without a preelection mutual security pact.

Failures in contemporary peace processes have often been exacerbated by the ill-considered or cynical attempts of incumbent authorities to manipulate the electoral process to achieve a victory over opponents at the polls that they were unable to achieve on the streets. Incumbents are expected to manipulate the rules to maximize their advantages when devising an electoral system, but should the international community wait until after the consequences of ill-chosen practices have occurred before intervening?[28] What responsibilities does the international community have in preventing parties from adopting practices that will in all likelihood result in conflict escalation?

The international community should more consistently focus on the electoral system choices of states embroiled in ethnic conflicts and develop more effective intervention strategies to help craft systems that are expected to ameliorate conflict rather than exacerbate it. The primary reason why electoral solutions to ethnic conflict, appropriately structured, are potentially useful tools of international diplomacy is that elections lend themselves to external observation and monitoring by the international community. In recent years, especially in elections that are the culmination of peace processes, elections have become internationalized in any event.

Election events such as these underscore the critical role of turning points in conflict dynamics and the challenge of identifying turning points in which parties may accept a power-sharing system as a temporary, transitional, or permanent solution to their struggles. Turning points often involve crises, which can give the international community a moment of opportunity for potentially fruitful intervention. How can mediators or disputants turn crises into opportunities? South Africa's experience again offers an example. In June 1992, after the collapse of constitutional talks and a sharp upsurge in political violence (especially the so-called Boipatong incident), the South African process seemed about to collapse. The principal negotiating parties were trapped in mutual recrimination regarding culpability for the violence and were deadlocked on constitutional issues.

In the wake of the Boipatong incident, the UN Secretary-General dispatched an envoy, Cyrus Vance, to investigate the violence and (implicitly) suggest ways it could be mitigated. Although Vance did not directly mediate on the constitutional issues on which the parties were deadlocked, the mission was successful in that the crisis provided an opportunity for intervention that did not previously exist. After the crisis, a stationary UN observation (not peacekeeping) team was deployed—the United Nations Mission in South Africa, UNOMSA—and virtually all observers agreed that the international presence helped cap escalating violence. When the next round of violence occurred in September 1992, the so-called Bisho incident, the principal parties to the talks were sufficiently shocked by the continuing escalation and soon thereafter sealed an important pact (the Record of Understanding) that laid the basis for a subsequent power-sharing agreement (Sisk 1995a:219–228).

The Vance mission was critical not because it directly produced a power-sharing outcome but, rather, because it helped create a situation in which further crises would bring the moderate parties, committed to negotiation, closer together rather than drive them farther apart. This example illustrates that though international intervention timed to follow a crisis may not in and of itself lead to a power-sharing arrangement, it may give parties sufficient "space" to conclude an agreement on their own.

The paradox of early intervention to promote power sharing when it is appropriate, however, is the following: At an early stage of conflict escalation, parties may not be sufficiently persuaded that special measures are needed to ameliorate the polarizing effects of ethnicity. They may well argue for regular majoritarian democracy. After an ethnic conflict turns violent, however, relations may be so damaged that parties are unwilling to share power in order to achieve mutual benefit, portending separation as the option of last resort. Precisely when and how the international community should incur the inherent risks of intervention in an ethnic conflict by encouraging parties to adopt power-sharing practices through inducements will always be a difficult judgment call, bedeviled by this paradox of timing. Like any other diplomatic initiative, the early promotion of power sharing has its inherent risks and costs, demands a coherent strategy, and usually requires a sustained commitment of diplomatic pressure; material resources are often required as well.

An example of the risk of interventions to promote power sharing is contemporary Kenya, where the entrenched president Daniel arap Moi has unveiled a plan to introduce ethnic federalism, or *majimboiism*, while leaving a strong presidency—and presumably Moi and his KANU (Kenya African National Union) successors—in place. Democratic opposition figures oppose the plan and fear that the regime will bring in outside experts, presumably proponents of federalism, to lend legitimacy to the manipulative scheme. Gilbert Khadiagala argues that Moi's ploy is an effort to drag "external actors into domestic debates on [the regime's] own terms" (1995:26). Such complicated situations underscore well the inherent risks of promoting presumably conflict-mitigating practices when their adoption may in fact have an opposite effect. The international community should be wary, for the landscape of power sharing can include myriad traps.

The problem is further complicated when a highly asymmetrical relationship exists among the conflicting parties, or when one party attempts to introduce a presumably conflict-mitigating practice in order to remain in power. For example, how can the international community intervene early in a relatively powerful state to prevent bloody conflict from emerging? In Nigeria, for example, annulment of the 1993 presidential election was especially devastating because the presumed winner, Moshood Abiola, was elected with Muslim support in northern states (including Kano, his opponent's home province) and with broader support among Nigeria's myriad ethnic groups, including the Igbo. The annulment of the election leads to the real possibility that Nigeria could polarize along religious lines and provide new incentives for Nigeria's (mostly Muslim) military leaders to bolster their position by mobilizing on religious terms (Suberu 1994).

Yet it is clear that little can be done to promote potentially viable alternatives to Nigeria's seemingly perpetual crisis of democratization—such as encouraging a government of national unity. Preventive diplomacy missions have been sent to Nigeria; the United States, for example, has dispatched highly respected envoys (former U.S. ambassador to the United Nations Donald McHenry as well as Rev. Jesse Jackson) to encourage fair trials for detained civic leaders and to urge the military regime to turn over power to civilians and once again attempt to democratize Nigeria. Some have suggested that power sharing in Nigeria should involve including the military in the ruling coalition or having a military-civilian dyarchy. A similar plan has been suggested for Burma; a nascent democratization process is potentially possible there.

Even at a late stage, intervention to promote power sharing can yield success. While in Cambodia it was impossible—and, many contend, undesirable—to bring the recalcitrant Khmer Rouge into the postelection governing coalition after its violent election boycott and its brutal past, the UN Secretary-General's special representative Yasushi Akashi was successful in forging a power-sharing pact—creating two prime ministerial positions—between the two largest vote getters in the election, the royalist FUNCIPEC and the defeated ruling Cambodian People's Party, which had threatened not to abide by the election results.

This last-minute diplomatic triumph suggests that although late intervention may be desirable, the parties may not accept power-sharing solutions until it is clear that their absence will lead to very violent and internationally unacceptable consequences. The Cambodian experience also demonstrates that in many instances of deep conflict, at least one significant party to the conflict will remain outside a power-sharing coalition, content to play the role of spoiler. It also makes clear that mediator staying power throughout the implementation phase of a settlement is a critical component of successful intervention.

Moreover, when the international community is likely to be asked to implement or guarantee the terms of a settlement, it will have a clear interest in its terms and the viability of its implementation. The 1993 Arusha Accord for peace in Rwanda was a seemingly fair power-sharing outcome to end the Tutsi insurgency against the primarily Hutu government of President Juvenal Habyarimana. Brokered by the government of Tanzania and the Organization of African Unity, the painstakingly crafted agreement provided a potentially workable exit to Rwanda's endemic ethnic strife. The pact created a sixty-forty Hutu-Tutsi division of power within the central government, entailing overrepresentation of the Tutsi (14 percent of the population) but reflective of the perceived balance of power among the groups. Implementation of the pact was to be overseen by a UN peacekeeping force. When Habyarimana was assassinated by Hutu extremists opposed to the power sharing and intergroup reconciliation, the stage was set for the fanning of communal flames and the genocide in April 1994. When the violence surged, most of the UN force was withdrawn, and a humanitarian catastrophe, still unresolved, ensued.[29] Rwanda, along with Somalia, now stands a symbol of the inability of the international community to effectively intervene in ethnic conflicts.

In addition to the paradox of timing, mediators also face a second challenge in advancing power sharing as the basis for a settlement—the difficulty of judging intentions. As with winner-take-all electoral systems, the question arises, How do mediators know whether a party agreeing to a power-sharing system is simply adjusting its tactics in pursuit of zero-sum goals or has actually changed from essentialist to pragmatic in its perception of opposing groups? How sustainable will the pact be in the long term? If a party's acquiescence to power sharing is only a tactical move, and the true intent of a party is to use other, more internationally acceptable means to subdue its opponents, then mediators cannot expect opposing parties to participate.

Stedman rightly notes that in the course of transitions, when disputants "insist on 'winner-take-all' arrangements, then they are looking at the settlement only from the tactical perspective of winning through agreement what they cannot win on the battlefield" (1995:57). The international community should seek to more consistently recognize situations in which parties' expectations of winning are ill founded and recognize when support for power-sharing practices is genuine or merely tactical. Intervention to promote power sharing usually entails choosing sides in a conflict. International actors backing power-sharing solutions to ethnic conflict not only end up choosing among disputants, some of whom may demand power sharing while others (often majority groups or incumbent officeholders) oppose, they also are often in the uncomfortable and difficult position of identifying and supporting moderates within an ethnic group—for example, within a government or party. Thus, advocating power sharing is a highly intrusive diplomatic option.

Policy Making and Power Sharing

Diplomats with difficult choices in complex conflicts, considering power sharing as a potential option to promote in efforts to end destructive ethnic strife, rightly ask straightforward questions about experiences with various forms of democratic practice in divided societies. What are the diagnostic tools for understanding an ethnic conflict? Under what conditions does power sharing work, and under what conditions does it fail? Under what conditions can parties to a conflict be expected to adopt power-sharing arrangements?

Is elite power sharing antidemocratic? Under what conditions do power-sharing systems entrench group identities and collapse into violent conflict? When do they lead eventually to more integrative and majoritarian patterns of democracy?

Similarly, they ask about their own role in helping ameliorate ethnic conflicts. What are the pitfalls of power sharing, and how can they be avoided in a given situation? How can the international community know whether power sharing is appropriate to violent conflict in a deeply divided society? If it is appropriate, what approach (consociational or integrative) and what combination of practices should be encouraged? At what stages in the escalation and de-escalation of a conflict should external parties such as mediators encourage or induce parties to adopt a power-sharing arrangement? What are the responsibilities of the international community when power-sharing experiments it has promoted fail?

Naturally, there are no simple answers to the questions posed above, but some conclusions can be drawn. A necessary condition for the mitigation of conflict in deeply divided societies is the existence, or creation, of a centrist core of moderates—drawn both from elites and from the broader civil society—that adheres to rules and norms of pragmatic coexistence with other groups and can withstand the pressures of extremist outbidders that seek to mobilize on divisive themes for their own power-seeking aims. The commitment to pragmatic coexistence must be *broad* (accepted by most disputants) and *deep* (accepted by political elites, their organizations, and constituencies in civil society). Absent such a commitment, the likely outcomes are violence, state collapse, state disintegration, or a civil war of attrition. When any of these outcomes occurs, or when parties to a conflict prefer to create the structures of separation (as in the Israeli-Palestinian conflict) rather than power sharing, the international community can and should countenance the creation of new states.

When a sufficiently cohesive cadre of moderates does exist, power sharing is a viable means of democratic conflict management. The term *power sharing* describes a wide variety of conflict-regulating practices, and each power-sharing system has its unique characteristics.

Though there is no single, transportable model of power sharing, there is a broad menu of conflict-regulating practices, institutions, and mechanisms. Moreover, power sharing may be appropriate as a transitional, confidence-building mechanism but not as a permanent solution to ethnic conflict management through democratic institutions. Whether the consociational or integrative power-sharing approach is better is highly conditional on the structure and dynamics of a given conflict situation and is ultimately a matter for the conflicting parties themselves to determine through negotiation. Chipman (1993:259–260) writes, "So much is contingent on circumstances of individual cases and the particular regional implications of different types of solutions. . . . In fact, there are few if any, instances in which selective choice from [a] menu is possible; more often, the whole menu needs to be applied, various elements in different places, but more or less simultaneously."

Power-sharing practices are likely to evolve in multiethnic societies if key political leaders are motivated to avoid violent conflict, prevent its escalation, or escape it through a mutually acceptable solution. Consociational conflict-regulating practices flow from protracted negotiation processes or transitions to democracy based on mutual security pacts, particularly those in which the parties' capabilities are in symmetry (Du Toit 1989b). Esman describes consociational arrangements as "a viable process of mutual deterrence" (1994:258). But because consociational power-sharing practices are based on elite coalescence and intergroup guarantees such as mutual vetoes, they are inherently limited as a system of deterrence. They face continual stress and are subject to breakdown when elite consensus is elusive or unsustainable or the practices are too rigid. Consociational power-sharing practices do offer conflicting parties a greater sense of security, but they may contain the seeds of their own demise. Deeply entrenched ethnic group rights and representation may in fact reify or exacerbate ethnic conflict.

On the other hand, opting for integrative practices requires a greater degree of trust among parties, which is often lacking, or more minimally enlightened self-interest among moderate leaders. Integrative practices are theoretically more attractive devices to, in the words of Horowitz, "[make] moderation pay" (1990b), but they may be unwieldy and parties may feel insufficiently secure to submit to the deep uncertainties of winning and losing in a more majoritarian electoral game. Moreover, the cohesion and crosscutting ties necessary for pluralistic forces to emerge may simply be insufficiently strong.

South Africa's ongoing experiment in power sharing offers a critical lesson in how, through protracted negotiations, parties can themselves derive a set of mutually beneficial conflict-regulating practices. Here, in a deeply divided society imbued with all of the centrifugal characteristics of destructive ethnic conflict during the apartheid years, the parties transformed their relationships and embraced a common set of practices deeply permeated with the ethos of living together. The November 1993 constitution struck a sufficiently fine balance between the rights of the majority and the insecurity of minorities to gain wide acceptance by the populace and strong backing by the international community. Although the consociational constraints of South Africa's current government of national unity—a five-year mandated grand coalition and especially a de facto minority veto at the local government level—will in all likelihood fall away in the final constitution now being deliberated and be replaced by more integrative conflict-regulating practices, including a slightly more majoritarian electoral system.

If the moderate center holds in South Africa, power sharing among elites will be seen as a critical stepping-stone toward more fully competitive and participatory democracy.[30] Yet even in South Africa, power sharing may have perverse consequences if the extraordinary measures taken to protect minorities—particularly the effective minority veto at the local government level—serve to preserve an unjust status quo, blocking sorely needed socioeconomic uplifting of the long-subjugated black majority.

Thus, conditional generalizations *can* be made about successful and unsuccessful power-sharing practices. Power sharing is successful in managing ethnic group tensions under the following conditions:

- A core of moderate, integrated elites has a deeply imbued sense of interdependence and shared or common destiny, and elites are genuinely representative of the groups and elements of civil society for whom they claim to speak.

- The practices adopted are flexible, sensitive to shifting demographics and to changing external and internal environments.
- The practices foster equitable resource distribution and manage change in a manner that does not create further grievances.
- The practices are indigenously arrived at and are not based on overwhelming external pressures or short-term, zero-sum expectations of the parties.
- Parties can eventually eschew the extraordinary measures that power-sharing practices entail and move toward a more integrative and liberal form of democracy in which the predominant divisions in society, over which control of the state is contested, are based not on the politics of identity but instead on perhaps equally divisive, but inherently more manageable, differences such as ideology or class (Przeworski 1991; Diamond 1990).

The initial experience of the Cold War era is that the liberal vision of removing ethnicity and identity as the basis of politics, relying on the principles of individual rights and majority rule, is unlikely to be realized soon in the vast majority of multiethnic states. The pervasiveness of identity politics, however regrettable, suggests that the promotion of power sharing in deeply divided multiethnic societies will be an increasingly important element in international attempts to prevent and manage the costly effects of violent ethnic conflict.

Notes

1. Introduction

1. Following Horowitz (1985:224), Esman (1994), Stavenhagen (1994), in this chapter I use the term *ethnic group* to encompass groups mobilized on the basis of identity or shared perceptions of common origin, which includes those organized around religion, culture, language, race, and caste. *Ethnic conflict* is defined in terms of political, social, or military confrontation, violent or nonviolent, in which disputants describe themselves in terms of race, language, religion, culture, or nationality or some combination of ascriptive criteria. See Anthony Smith (1993) for a list of ten criteria for a group to qualify as an ethnic group according to this common usage of the term.

2. Ted Robert Gurr, in a global survey of minority groups at risk, has identified some 5,000 distinct ethnic groups and pinpoints about 80 significant and ongoing hot ethnic conflicts, 35 of which are in an incipient or active stage of civil war (Gurr 1993).

3. On arguments for and against secession, see Buchheit (1978) and Horowitz (1985:229–288). See also Allen Buchanan, *Secession: The Morality of Political Divorce* (Boulder, Colo.: Westview, 1991).

4. The principle of self-determination in international law is, as Ralph Steinhart (1994) argues, at a "legislative turning point." Although it is not likely to be equated with secession, its application is undergoing significant change with the end of decolonization. The standard interpretation of the term, which grants self-determination to former colonized peoples, is no longer applicable, requiring either the abandonment of the principle or new interpretations and applications. For a review of the contemporary debate on the principle of self-determination in international law, see Steinhart (1994), Hannum (1989, 1990), and Halperin, Scheffer, and Small (1992).

5. See Boutros-Ghali (1995). In this book, I employ the definition of democracy in terms of what Robert Dahl (1971) has termed "polyarchy," that is, a political system that provides meaningful and extensive *contestation* among individuals and groups, particularly political parties; political *participation* in selecting leaders and policies; and the protection of *political liberties* to ensure the integrity of contestation and participation. Contestation, participation, and liberties are values to be maximized in a democratic political system; that is, the degree of democracy in a society is a question of the extent to which these values are maximized.

2. Ethnic Conflict: Approaches, Patterns, and Dynamics

1. See the bibliographies in Esman (1994) and Brown (1993) for a list of some of the recent literature on ethnic conflict.

2. Primordialists do not suggest that ethnic identities cannot change or that the boundaries of ethnic groups may not expand or contract, but this orientation does suggest that the ability to transcend or escape ethnic identity is limited and that ethnic groups will act to ensure collective survival (Geertz 1963). Thus, ethnic group identities flow from an extended kinship bond, sharing common behaviors and transmitting across generations basic norms and customs, or ethnic culture (Smith 1981). Others, such as Barth (1969), focus on ethnic groups' formation of boundaries within society, which boundaries may be relatively rigid or open. Finally, there are the strong linkages many ethnic groups associate, in a primal way, with territory, leading some authors to suggest an ecological basis of ethnic group variation, particularly when territory is contested or where scarce resources may heighten competition (Banton 1983).

3. Scholars in the rational choice tradition derived from economics argue that individuals will coalesce to act collectively in value-maximizing pursuits and will participate or abstain from ethnic collective action on the basis of their own individual interests and ambitions. The interests of an ethnic group, according to this explanation, are but the sum of the individual interests of its members, a means to an end but not an end unto itself (Rogowski 1985:87–108; Meadwell 1989, 1991; Levi and Hechter 1985). Thus, ethnicity is a chimera that obscures the individual rational pursuit of goods through collective action.

4. Modern social science describes divisions within a society in terms of "cleavages," such as language, ethnicity, religion, race, region, gender, or class (Rae and Taylor 1970; Lijphart 1977a:71–81).

5. On voluntary versus ascriptive associations in civil society, see Chazan (1982).

6. Gurr (1993:15–23) distinguishes between "national peoples" (ethno-national groups or indigenous peoples) and "minority groups" (ethnoclasses, militant sects, and dominant, advantaged, or disadvantaged "communal contenders").

7. Personal communication with the author, August 21, 1995.

8. The problem of ethnic outbidding is not only one of errant or manipulative political leadership, but also a more general one of collective action. For if appeals to ethnic solidarity do not resonate among the populace, political leaders would have very little incentive to resort to them

9. Esman (1994:2–3), in a useful typology, identifies three sources of multiethnic pluralism in contemporary states: conquest, decolonization, and migration. He also identifies an important and critical distinction between homeland societies, that is, groups that claim a historical right to specific territory, and diaspora groups that have migrated to places other than their traditional homeland either voluntarily or involuntarily (6–9).

10. On the terminological difference between a state, a nation, and an ethnic group, see Connor (1978) and Ra'anan (1991).

11. For a recent treatment of these issues, see Coakley (1994).

12. On the internationalization of ethnic conflict, see Suhrke and Noble (1977), Brown (1993), and Esman (1994). For an in-depth treatment of this theme in South Asia, see De Silva and May (1991).

13. Walker and Stern (1993:7), summarizing a U.S. National Research Council workshop on balancing and sharing political power in multiethnic societies, offer a useful typology of the types of ethnic conflicts in the former Soviet Union: interstate conflicts, indigenous minorities, settler communities, forcible relocation, formerly autonomous regions, and communal violence.

14. Personal communication with the author, August 30, 1995.

15. For more on techniques and models of early warning for ethnic conflict escalation, see the July 1994 special edition of the *Journal of Ethno-Development*, "Early Warning of Communal Conflicts and Humanitarian Crises" (vol. 4, no. 1).

16. See also Posen (1993).

17. This is not to say that a conflict cannot escalate even as parties gather around the negotiating table. The parties in the former Yugoslavia have been negotiating under international auspices even as the conflict escalated vertically and horizontally. So, too, have the parties to the Sudanese conflict. Moreover, even as negotiations begin in earnest and the conflict moves toward settlement, violence can continue and even increase. This was the case in South Africa, when even after formal negotiations

began, violence was used as a "beyond the table tactic" by parties to the conflict (Sisk 1993b).

18. Waterman (1993:292) argues that "civil wars are conflicts over political order," and settlements in them entail the "re-creation of the conditions for a viable, common political order."

3. Democracy and Its Alternatives in Deeply Divided Societies

1. Ian Lustick (1979, 1980) refers to such practices that subjugate outgroups in a society as a "control" model of intergroup relations, citing Israel and apartheid South Africa as preeminent examples of this approach.

2. Personal communication with the author, August 25, 1995.

3. Another way to think about the "hegemonic exchange" approach is the term *concertation*, or "organized efforts at concerted decision-making where interested parties are explicitly included in the bargaining process and often in implementation as well" (Rothchild and Foley 1988:258).

4. Horowitz, however, disagrees with this analysis, suggesting that "many one-party states *said* they were inclusive but were actually ethnocracies (states ruled by one ethnic group: Ivory Coast, Cameroon, Kenya, Uganda under Amin)." Personal communication with the author, August 21, 1995.

5. Horowitz (1985:588–592) has a particularly well-developed argument on the often-destructive consequences of secessionist attempts in deeply divided societies, which, like Lijphart, he argues is viable only as "a fallback position" (Horowitz 1991:132).

6. Political culture theorists (Almond and Verba 1963) focus on the beliefs and norms of participation and tolerance associated with Western society and include social homogeneity as a prerequisite for successful democracy—in sum, value consensus, crosscutting allegiances, and moderate attitudes must exist *prior* to the introduction of open electoral competition. When these cultural attributes are absent, so too is democracy. For a recent defense of the political culture approach, see Lipset (1990), who argues that Protestantism and a previous British colonial connection best explain the presence or absence of democratic practices.

7. See the essays in Montville (1990) for further elaboration of these themes.

8. Personal communication with the author, August 30, 1995.

9. The absence of floating voters is a critical assumption for antimajoritarians, one that I return to in the section titled "Choosing an

Appropriate Electoral System." In defense of the assumption, Nordlinger writes: "Orthodox democratic theory, which presupposes alternating or shifting majorities, is certainly not applicable to divided societies. Given the conflict's intensity, individuals belonging to a particular segment or conflict group will be adamantly and emotionally attached to 'their' political party or parties. And in this kind of electoral arena party leaders rarely seek to broaden their appeals in order to win the support of intractable individuals belonging to the opposing segment" (1972:34–35).

10. Bogdanor summarizes the scholarly consensus: "Where . . . the basic cleavage is ethnic, religious, territorial, or tribal, the plurality method will emphasize concentrations of support, and it will tend to emphasize territorial cleavages at the expense of socio-economic ones. Plurality and majority methods will work less successfully in deeply divided or plural societies than in homogenous ones" (1987:195). This consensus is by no means unanimous, however, a point that I return to in chapter 4.

11. See Lijphart (1977a:25–28, 114–118) and Horowitz (1985:629–630) for critiques of majoritarianism in deeply divided societies. Horowitz (1985:333–364) provides a lengthy analysis of the acute problems of ethnic party systems.

12. The coalescent-adversarial distinction is Lijphart's (1977a:25).

13. The literature on consociational democracy is well developed. While the groundbreaking work is Lijphart's, particularly his 1977 book *Democracy in Plural Societies* (1977a), many other scholars have contributed to the approach. First, consociationalism has its antecedents in the earlier work of Lijphart (1968), which termed the approach "the politics of accommodation." Landmark works in the school include Daalder (1971), McRae (1974), and Pappalardo (1981). Several scholars, led by Jurg Steiner, have sought to extend the consociational approach to a broader framework of decision making in coalitions. See Steiner's articles (1981a, 1981b), as well as his earlier book on Switzerland. Other scholars, such as Lembruch and Schmitter, have related consociational theory to the corporatist model, arguing that these approaches are complementary; their views are best stated in Lembruch and Schmitter (1979). Lijphart (1985) catalogs and responds to critics of the consociational approach.

14. Horowitz does not consider the Malaysian and Lebanese experiences to have been consociational, arguing that "neither was a grand coalition, neither had a proportional electoral system, and neither had a minority veto. In neither case did the ruling coalition ever represent the segments as such, only parts of the segments. In fact, none of the (only) four cases cited by Lijphart in his 1977 book as a consociational regime in a severely divided society was one." Personal communication with the author, August

25, 1995. For more on Horowitz's views on this issue, see his book *Ethnic Groups in Conflict* (1985:575–576).

15. Grand coalitions can occur either in the cabinet or parliamentary systems, in "grand councils," or as a grand coalition of a president and senior executives in presidential systems (Lijphart 1977b:118).

16. Personal communication with the author, August 30, 1995.

17. For instance, despite the failure of power sharing in Cyprus in the early 1960s, power sharing appears to be the only solution to that conflict as evidenced by the substance of the UN Secretary-General's 1992 "Set of Ideas" for Cyprus (see chapter 6).

18. Personal communication with the author, August 21, 1995.

4. Typology of Conflict-Regulating Practices

1. The author's study of democratization in South Africa (Sisk 1995a) shows how the power-sharing structures of the 1993 constitution were the outcome of a negotiation process and represents a fair compromise given the parties' interests and ideologies and the relative balance of power among them.

2. On the latter, see Boyle and Hadden (1994).

3. Boundary demarcation is inevitably a critical and sensitive issue in creating or amending federal systems. On criteria for determining "just" boundaries, see Walker and Stern (1993:4).

4. An example is the conflict-mitigating effect that South Africa's choice for regionalism has had. In the 1994 election the primarily white National Party, supported by a majority of the so-called Colored community (mulattos), won a province, as did the primarily Zulu-based Inkatha Freedom Party.

5. For ten yardsticks to measure federal-subfederal relations, see Duchacek (1987:188–276).

6. On the management of ethnoterritorial conflict in Western states, see Rudolph and Thompson (1989).

7. See Stephen Buckley, "Ethiopia Takes a New Ethnic Tack: Deliberately Divisive," *Washington Post*, June 18, 1995, A21.

8. Lijphart does argue (1977a:33) that types of presidentialism and consociationalism are compatible, although the type of decision-making structure he advocates (grand coalition) is clearly different from the broad-based presidential model advocated by Horowitz.

9. Federal Republic of Nigeria, *The Constitution of the Federal Republic of Nigeria Promulgation Decree* (1989), Article 131 (1)(a).

10. Personal communication with the author September 21, 1995.

11. For a thorough discussion of the communal proportional representation principle, see Duchacek (1987:108ff.).

12. Personal communication with the author, July 24, 1995.

13. See Samia (forthcoming) and Maila (1992) for a review of the terms of the Taif Accord, the power-sharing arrangements agreed on in the context of the experiences with earlier Lebanese efforts to manage confessional differences, and the implications for conflict resolution. Samia concludes that the agreement should not be considered a final statement of intergroup relations in Lebanon, but that "amending, reviewing, reconsidering, and rewriting some [of its key terms] to recreate balance and equity is a virtue."

14. See Lijphart (1994a:139–152) for the effects of political engineering on the degree of proportionality, the party system, and the nature of majority victory.

15. See the essays in Lijphart and Grofman (1986: esp. pts. 1 and 2) for a discussion of the varieties of PR and PR list systems.

16. Given sufficiently high district magnitude (number of candidates per district), PR systems can yield results with very low measures of vote-to-seat distortions. Generally, the higher the district magnitude the greater the proportionality.

17. Examples of polarized pluralism include Italy (before recent changes in its electoral system) and Israel.

18. See Taagepera and Shugart (1989) for a thorough discussion of alternative preference voting systems.

19. The last condition is critical. If the constituencies are too divided and there exists no sentiment for accommodation in the electorate, vote pooling cannot establish it.

20. Lijphart notes that "Malaysia has managed as a power-sharing system in spite of, not because of, the plurality system. Some form of PR would have been more straightforward." Personal communication with the author, August 25, 1995.

21. Personal communication with the author, August 21, 1995.

22. Andrew Reynolds points out in personal communication with the author (September 26, 1995) that had the South Africans opted for a PR representation threshold of up to 5 percent, significant parties (notably the Democratic Party, the Pan-Africanist Congress, the Freedom Front, and the African Christian Democratic Party) would not have won seats in parliament.

23. See Samarasinghe and Coughlan (1991).

24. *Constitution of India*, Article 46. This declaration is supported by other articles in the Indian constitution that proclaim the right to equality and a prohibition on state discrimination against citizens on the grounds of religion, race, caste, sex, or place of birth [Articles 15(2) and 16(2)]. The constitution backs up these directives with the reservation of seats for the disadvantaged groups for at least ten years beyond adoption in 1949, but these reservations have been regularly extended.

25. *Constitution of the Republic of Namibia*, Chapter 11, 9–101.

26. *Constitution of the Federal Republic of Nigeria Promulgation Decree*, Article 16(d). The crosscutting-divisions approach is not only embraced as an objective but mandated in the party system as well. Article 220 requires a maximum of two state-registered political parties in the Third Republic, and the parties' "name, . . . emblem or motto [can] not contain any ethnic or religious connotation or give the appearance that the activities of the association are confined to a part only of the geographical area of Nigeria" [Article 220(e)].

27. In South Africa's attempts to foster a spirit of national reconciliation after apartheid, an agreement was reached in the 1993 interim constitution to adopt two national anthems. The apartheid-era national anthem "Die Stem" (the voice) was dear to the nationalist Afrikaners that built and maintained apartheid, and it was a stark symbol of oppression to the black majority. Likewise, the liberation anthem "N'kosi Sikele Afrika" (God bless Africa) was the rallying cry of the antiapartheid resistance movement, and as a symbol of resistance to the old order it was despised by many white South Africans. Rather than adopt a new anthem, South Africa adopted them both for the postapartheid transitional period; both anthems are sung at official gatherings. During the campaign leading up to the 1994 election, "N'kosi" was often sung at the rallies of the erstwhile governing National Party to woo the support of potential black voters. Similarly, South Africa's new multicolor flag, drawn from the official colors of South Africa's major parties by a multiparty committee, has surprisingly received widespread acceptance as the symbol of the new, inclusive, multiethnic order.

5. Power Sharing and Peace Processes

1. Personal communication with the author, August 25, 1995.

2. On the evolution of the conflict in Burundi and for details on the terms of the Convention of Government, which gives the Tutsi-based opposition a 45-percent share in government (Tutsis comprise about 14 percent of the population but control the military), see the report by Minority Rights Group International, "Burundi: Breaking the Cycle of Violence" (Minority Rights Group International, 1995).

3. Stephen Buckley, "Killings Derail Rwandan Reconciliation," *Washington Post*, April 25, 1995, A1, A13.

4. On the development and operation of this decision rule in South Africa's 1992–1994 constitutional negotiations, see Sisk (1995a:200–248).

6. International Intervention and Power Sharing

1. Personal communication with the author, August 21, 1995

2. For a review of issues related to international intervention in civil wars, especially issues related to UN peacekeeping operations, see Weiss (1994), Stedman (1995), and Cooper and Berdal (1993).

3. For a comprehensive treatment of issues related to preventive diplomacy with special reference to the United States, see Lund (1996).

4. "Supplement to the Agenda for Peace: Position Paper of the Secretary-General on the Occasion of the Fiftieth Anniversary of the United Nations," A/50/60, S/1995/a, January 3, 1995, 5.

5. Personal communication with the author, September 6, 1995. I am indebted to Pierre du Toit for pointing out this prior, fundamental question and for directing me to Dahl's discussion of this problem.

6. "Supplement," 12 (see n. 4).

7. Horowitz writes, "In many countries of Africa, Asia, Europe and the Former Soviet Union, a major reason for the failure of democratization is ethnic conflict" (1993:18).

8. On the role of "turning points" in negotiations, see Druckman (1986).

9. Personal communication with the author, August 21, 1995.

10. Interview by the author with African National Congress negotiator Kader Asmal, April 15, 1991.

11. See "Sudan: Ending the War, Moving Talks Forward," United States Institute of Peace Special Report, April 1994.

12. "Report of the Co-Chairman [of the International Conference on Former Yugoslavia] on Progress in Development of a Constitution for Bosnia and Herzegovina," October 25, 1992, Annex.

13. Väyrynen and Leatherman correctly assert that "particularly challenging to the international community are policies of ethnic decimation or ethnic cleansing in which parties to the conflict may also use [violence beyond] the negotiating table to reach their aims; as in the case of the Bosnian war, international efforts to reach a settlement to the conflict have been seen as legitimizing territorial gains achieved by means of genocide" (1995:12).

14. Croatian Serbs would have been provided substantial autonomy, including their own flag, currency, executive, parliament, and police force. In exchange for autonomy, the Serbs would have yielded territory to central government control in areas where prior to the war they were not a majority.

15. *New York Times,* January 30, 1995, A3.

16. The Secretary-General's proposals include the following elements [S/23780, 1992], which appear here in detail as an illustration of the degree of specificity an external formula can provide.

> 1. *Overall objectives.* The aim of the overall framework is a "new partnership and a new constitution" for Cyprus on a bicommunal, federal basis; it would be "bizonal" in territorial terms. The agreement recognizes that "Cyprus is the common home of the Greek Cypriot community and of the Turkish Cypriot community and that their relationship is not one of majority and minority but one of two communities in the federal republic of Cyprus. It safeguards the cultural, religious, political, social, and linguistic identity of each community." The political equality of the two communities is guaranteed, but numerical participation in the federal government is not implied. The "Set of Ideas" includes a federal government that ensures the effective participation of the communities and the power of communities to veto matters that directly affect them. The following guiding principles will reign: the federal state will be bicommunal and bizonal; separate referendums will bring a new federal constitution into force; the federal republic's sovereignty will be indivisible; the federal government will be secular; "special ties of friendship" with Greece and Turkey will be retained; both Greek and Turkish will be official languages, and English may be used; new flags and holidays will be agreed on; the federated states will have identical powers and functions; security, law, and justice will be the responsibility of the federal government; and the states will cooperate with respect to the preservation of religious sites.
>
> 2. *Constitutional arrangements.* The central government will have powers over monetary policy; customs and international trade; airports and ports; federal taxation; immigration and citizenship; defense (a

separate treaty on defense is envisaged); federal judiciary and police; postal and telecommunications services; and public health, environment, and natural resources. All other powers are vested in the states. The lower house will be bicommunal with a 70:30 ratio of Greek Cypriots to Turkish Cypriots, and the upper house will have a 50:50 ratio; special majorities will be required for passing legislation. The federal executive will be shared, in that if the president is of one community, the vice president must be of the other; the cabinet is constituted on a 7:3 ratio of Greek Cypriots to Turkish Cypriots. A bill of fundamental rights will safeguard community rights.

3. *Territorial adjustments.* The "Set of Ideas" includes a map that delineates two federated states (adhering to a set of specific and lengthy criteria laid out in earlier Secretary-General reports on Cyprus) and provides for a pragmatic territorial adjustment. The adjustments would enlarge the Turkish Cypriot area but would make adjustments in both directions.

4. *Displaced persons.* The right of return and the right to property of the estimated 160,000 Greek Cypriots and 45,000 Turkish Cypriots displaced in the conflict of 1974 are guaranteed. A number of practical difficulties have arisen with regard to this provision.

5. *Transitional arrangements.* After a referendum in both areas approving of the overall framework, an eighteen-month transition period is envisaged. Bicommunal committees on each of the specific issues covered by the accord will be organized, with the assistance of, and verification by, the United Nations. During the transitional period, current arrangements for the administration of day-to-day affairs will be maintained, as will existing external affairs (with provision for joint delegations to international meetings). Current legal systems are maintained unless they violate the overall agreement. During the transitional period, the following measures to promote "goodwill and close relations" will be implemented: the free flow of persons and goods, services, capital, communication, and international assistance will be ensured; all travel restrictions will be lifted; restrictions on the movement of tourists will be lifted; international sports and cultural boycotts will be lifted; the district of Varosha will come under UN administration; all military modernization and enhancement programs will cease, and both sides will cooperate with the UN Peacekeeping Force in Cyprus (UNICYP) in extending the redeployment of troops near the buffer zone; the free movement of UNICYP throughout the country will be

ensured; school textbooks will be re-written by a bicommunal committee to promote intercommunal harmony; the water question will be considered by a bicommunal committee, as will historical and religious sites; a bicommunal committee will undertake a population census; and an investigation into missing persons will be undertaken.

17. See John J. Maresca, "War in the Caucasus: A Proposal for the Settlement Over the Conflict of Nagorno-Karabakh," United States Institute of Peace Special Report, July 1994.

18. The Framework Document envisages the Northern Ireland Assembly, as well as new North-South (Belfast-Dublin) and East-West (Anglo-Irish) institutions. The Framework Document is riddled with references to "mutual consent" as the operational decision rule and multiple mechanisms for systematic protection of human rights, including "cultural and confessional" rights. For a detailed discussion of the plan's provisions, see *The Irish Emigrant*, issue 421, February 27, 1995.

19. As part of the negotiations leading to the Lusaka Protocol, Savimbi was reportedly offered the post of vice president, but, preferring to remain outside, the UNITA leader declined, raising concerns about his intentions in agreeing to the pact and the longer-term viability of the accords. One important source of leverage was the UN mediator's unofficial condition that a renewed mandate of the peacekeeping force in Angola (UNAVEM), which both parties desired, was contingent on a detailed settlement. Influence exerted by South African president Nelson Mandela on the Angolan leadership was an equally important factor.

20. *Washington Post* reporter Paul Taylor suggests that Savimbi realized the power-sharing pact was "the best he could get" and also raises the specter that by staying outside, the UNITA leader may seek to further destabilize the agreement despite public commitments to the contrary. See Taylor, "Angolan Civil War Rivals Embrace, Pledge to Work as Partners in Peace," *Washington Post*, May 7, 1995, A32.

21. Declaration on the Rights of Persons Belonging to National or Ethnic, Religious or Linguistic Minorities (Minority Rights Declaration), GA Res. 47/135, December 18, 1992.

22. See Stephen Kinzer, "We Can Work it Out," *New York Times*, March 26, 1995, E4.

23. Personal communication with the author, August 30, 1995.

24. "Report from the CSCE Meeting on National Minorities," *Helsinki Monitor* 2 (4), 1991. For further discussion of the OSCE rules, see Steinhart (1994:30–31).

25. On the linkages between assistance and ethnic conflict management, see Walker and Stern (1993:177).

26. See David Binder and Barbara Crosette, "As Ethnic Wars Multiply, U.S. Strives for a Policy," *New York Times*, February 4, 1993, A1, 14.

27. Personal communication with the author, August 30, 1995.

28. On the ways in which incumbent governments can manipulate electoral systems rules, see Brady and Mo (1992).

29. See Human Rights Watch (1995:1–29) for details on the events leading up to and following the genocide in Rwanda and the international community's response.

30. Burton and Higley argue that transitions to democracy always begin as elite endeavors, but eventually are broadened to inculcate democratic values more deeply in society (Burton and Higley 1987; Higley and Burton 1989).

References

Almond, Gabriel, and Sidney Verba. 1963. *The Civic Culture: Political Attitudes and Democracy in Five Nations.* Princeton, N.J.: Princeton University Press.

Arrow, Kenneth. 1963. *Social Choice and Individual Values.* New Haven, Conn.: Yale University Press.

Azar, Edward, and John W. Burton. 1986. *International Conflict Resolution: Theory and Practice.* Boulder, Colo.: Lynne Rienner.

Banton, Michael. 1983. *Racial and Ethnic Competition.* Cambridge, U.K.: Cambridge University Press.

Barry, Brian. 1975. "Review Article: Political Accommodation and Consociational Democracy." *British Journal of Political Science* 5(October): 477–505.

Barth, F. 1969. *Ethnic Groups and Boundaries.* Oslo, Norway: Universitetsforlaget.

Bercovitch, Jacob. 1989. "International Dispute Mediation: A Comparative Empirical Analysis." In *Mediation Research*, Kenneth Kressel, ed. San Francisco: Jossey-Bass.

———. 1992. "Mediators and Mediation Strategies in International Relations." *Negotiation Journal* 8(2):99–112.

Bogdanor, Vernon, ed. 1987. *The Blackwell Encyclopedia of Political Institutions.* New York: Basil Blackwell.

Boutros-Ghali, Boutros. 1992. *An Agenda For Peace.* New York: United Nations.

———. 1995. "Democracy: A Newly Recognized Imperative." *Global Governance* 1(1):3–13.

Boyle, Kevin, and Tom Hadden. 1994. *Northern Ireland: The Choice.* London: Penguin Books.

Brady, David, and Jongryn Mo. 1992. "Electoral Systems and Institutional Choice: A Case Study of the 1988 Korean Elections." *Comparative Political Studies* 24(2):405–429.

Brass, Paul. 1990. *The Politics of India Since Independence*. Cambridge, U.K.: Cambridge University Press.

Brass, Paul, ed. 1985. *Ethnic Groups and the State*. Totowa, N.J.: Barnes and Noble Books.

Brown, Michael, ed. 1993. *Ethnic Conflict and International Security*. Princeton, N.J.: Princeton University Press.

Buchheit, Lee C. 1978. *Secession: The Legitimacy of Self-Determination*. New Haven, Conn.: Yale University Press.

Burton, Michael G., and John Higley. 1987. "Elite Settlements." *American Sociological Review* 52:295–307.

Call, Chuck. 1995. "Power Sharing in Latin America: Revisiting Colombia's National Front." Unpublished manuscript.

Chazan, Naomi. 1982. "The New Politics of Participation in Colonial Africa." *Comparative Politics* 14(2):169–189.

Chernick, Marc W. 1991. "Insurgency and Negotiations: Defining the Boundaries of the Political Regime in Colombia." Ph.D. dissertation, Columbia University.

Chipman, John. 1993. *Managing the Politics of Parochialism*. In *Ethnic Conflict and International Security*, Michael Brown, ed. Princeton, N.J.: Princeton University Press.

Coakley, John. 1994. *The Territorial Management of Ethnic Conflict*. London: Frank Cass.

Conflict Management Group. 1993. *Methods and Strategies in Conflict Prevention*. Report of an Expert Consultation on the Activities of the CSCE High Commissioner on National Minorities. Cambridge, Mass.: Conflict Management Group.

Connor, Walker. 1978. "A Nation is a Nation, Is a State, Is an Ethnic Group, Is a . . ." *Ethnic and Racial Studies* 50:377–400.

Cooper, Robert, and Mats Berdal. 1993. "Outside Intervention in Ethnic Conflict." In *Ethnic Conflict and International Security*, Michael Brown, ed. Princeton, N.J.: Princeton University Press.

Daalder, Hans. 1971. "On Building Consociational Nations: The Cases of the Netherlands and Switzerland." *Legislative Studies Quarterly* 3(2):11–25.

Dahl, Robert. 1971. *Polyarchy: Participation and Opposition*. New Haven: Yale University Press.

———. 1973. "Introduction." In *Regimes and Oppositions*, Robert Dahl, ed. New Haven, Conn.: Yale University Press.

———. 1989. *Democracy and its Critics*. New Haven: Yale University Press.

Das Gupta, Jyotirindra. 1989. "India: Democratic Becoming and Combined Development." In *Democracy in Developing Countries, Vol. 3, Asia*, Larry Diamond, Juan Linz, and Seymour Martin Lipset, eds. Boulder, Colo.: Lynne Rienner.

De Nevers, Renee. 1993. "Democratization and Ethnic Conflict." In *Ethnic Conflict and International Security*, Michael Brown, ed. Princeton, N.J.: Princeton University Press.

De Silva, K. M., and R. J. May. 1991. *Internationalization of Ethnic Conflict*. London: Pinter Publications.

Diamond, Larry. 1990. "Three Paradoxes of Democracy." *Journal of Democracy* 1(3):48–60.

Diamond, Larry, and Marc F. Plattner. 1994. "Introduction." In *Nationalism, Ethnic Conflict, and Democracy*, Larry Diamond and Marc F. Plattner, eds. Baltimore, Md.: Johns Hopkins University Press.

Druckman, Daniel. 1986. "Stages, Turning Points, and Crises." *Journal of Conflict Resolution* 30:327–360.

Duchacek, Ivo. 1973. *Power Maps: Comparative Politics of Constitutions*. Santa Barbara, Calif.: ABC Clio Press.

———. 1987. *Comparative Federalism: The Territorial Dimension of Politics*. Lanham, Md.: University Press of America.

Duffy, Gavin, and Natalie Frensley. 1989. "Community Conflict Processes: Mobilization and Demobilization in Northern Ireland." Program on the Analysis and Resolution of Conflicts, Maxwell School of Citizenship and Public Affairs, Syracuse University (Working Paper #13).

Du Toit, Pierre. 1989a. "Bargaining About Bargaining: Inducing the Self-Negating Prediction in Deeply Divided Societies: The Case of South Africa." *Journal of Conflict Resolution* 33:210–233.

———. 1989b. "Consociational Democracy and Bargaining Power." *Comparative Politics* 17:419–430.

Duverger, Maurice. 1964. *Political Parties*. Barbara and Robert North, trans. New York: John Wiley & Sons.

Elazar, Daniel. 1985. "Constitution-Making: The Preeminently Political Act." In *The Politics of Constitutional Change in Industrial Nations: Redesigning the State*, Simeon and Banting, eds. London: Macmillan Press.

Esman, Milton J. 1986. "Ethnic Politics and Economic Power." *Comparative Politics* 19(4):395–418.

———. 1994. *Ethnic Politics*. Ithaca, N.Y.: Cornell University Press.

Geertz, Clifford, ed. 1963. *Old Societies and New States: The Quest for Modernity in Asia and Africa*. New York: Free Press of Glencoe.

George, Alexander L. 1993a. *Bridging the Gap: Theory and Practice in Foreign Policy*. Washington, D.C.: United States Institute of Peace Press.

———. 1993b. *Forceful Persuasion: Coercive Diplomacy as an Alternative to War*. Washington, D.C.: United States Institute of Peace Press.

Gurr, Ted Robert. 1993. *Minorities at Risk: A Global View of Ethnopolitical Conflicts* Washington, D.C.: United States Institute of Peace Press.

Halperin, Morton H., and David J. Scheffer, with Patricia L. Small. 1992. *Self-Determination in the New World Order*. Washington, D.C.: Carnegie Endowment for International Peace.

Hannum, Hurst. 1989. "The Limits of Sovereignty and Majority Rule: Minorities, Indigenous Peoples and the Rights to Autonomy." In *New Directions in Human Rights*, Ellen Lutz, Hurst Hannum, and Kathryn J. Burke, eds. Philadelphia, Pa.: University of Pennsylvania Press.

———. 1990. *Autonomy, Sovereignty, and Self-Determination*. Philadelphia, Pa.: University of Pennsylvania Press.

Hardgrave, Robert L., Jr. 1994. "India: The Dilemmas of Diversity." In *Nationalism, Ethnic Conflict, and Democracy*, Larry Diamond and Marc F. Plattner, eds. Baltimore, Md.: Johns Hopkins University Press.

Hartlyn, Jonathan. 1988. *The Politics of Coalition Rule in Colombia*. Cambridge, U.K.: Cambridge University Press.

Helman, Gerald B., and Steven R. Ratner. 1992–1993. "Saving Failed States." *Foreign Policy* 89:3–20.

Higley, John, and Michael G. Burton. 1989. "The Elite Variable in Democratic Transitions and Breakdowns." *American Sociological Review* 54:17–32.

Horowitz, Donald. 1985. *Ethnic Groups in Conflict*. Berkeley: University of California Press.

———. 1990a. "Comparing Democratic Systems." *Journal of Democracy* 1(4):73–79.

———. 1990b. "Making Moderation Pay." In *Conflict and Peacemaking in Multiethnic Societies*, Joseph Montville, ed. Lexington, Mass.: Lexington Books.

———. 1991. *A Democratic South Africa? Constitutional Engineering in a Divided Society*. Berkeley: University of California Press.

———. 1993. "Democracy in Divided Societies." *Journal of Democracy* 4(4):18–38.

Human Rights Watch. 1995. *Playing the 'Communal Card': Communal Violence and Human Rights.* New York: Human Rights Watch.

Hume, Cameron. 1994. *Ending Mozambique's War: The Role of Mediation and Good Offices.* Washington, D.C.: United States Institute of Peace Press.

Huntington, Samuel P. 1972. "Foreword." In *Conflict Resolution in Divided Societies*, Eric Nordlinger. Occasional Papers in International Affairs No. 29, Harvard University.

————. 1981. "Reform and Stability in a Modernizing, Multi-Ethnic Society." *Politikon* 8(2):8–26.

Kaase, Max. 1986. "Personalized Proportional Representation: The 'Model' of the West German Electoral System." In *Choosing an Electoral System: Issues and Alternatives*, Arend Lijphart and Bernard Grofman, eds. New York: Praeger.

Kampelman, Max. 1993. "Secession and the Right to Self-Determination: An Urgent Need to Harmonize Principle with Pragmatism." *Washington Quarterly* 5(2):5–12.

Karl, Terry Lynn. 1990. "Dilemmas of Democratization in Latin America." *Comparative Politics* 23(1):1–21.

Khadiagala, Gilbert M. 1995. "Preventive Diplomacy in Africa: The Kenyan Case." Paper prepared for presentation at the conference "Preventive Diplomacy in Africa: The Challenge of Prescription," The Paul Nitze School of Advanced International Studies, Johns Hopkins University, Washington, D.C., April 7–8.

Kriesberg, Louis. 1989. "Timing and the Initiation of De-Escalation Moves." *Negotiation Journal* 3(4):375–384.

Lardeyret, Guy. 1991. "The Problem with PR." *Journal of Democracy* 2(3):30–35.

Lembruch, Gerhard, and Phillippe C. Schmitter, eds. 1979. *Trends Toward Corporatist Intermediation.* Beverly Hills, Calif.: Sage.

Levi, Margaret, and Michael Hechter. 1985. "A Rational Choice Approach to the Rise and Decline of Ethnoregional Political Parties." In *New Nationalisms of the Developed West*, Edward Tiryakian and Ronald Rogowski, eds. Boston: Allen & Ulwin.

Lijphart, Arend. 1968. *The Politics of Accommodation: Pluralism and Democracy in the Netherlands.* Berkeley: University of California Press.

————. 1969. "Consociational Democracy." *World Politics* 4(January): 207–225.

————. 1977a. *Democracy in Plural Societies.* New Haven, Conn.: Yale University Press.

————. 1977b. "Majority Rule versus Consociationalism in Deeply Divided Societies." *Politikon* 4(December):113–126.

————. 1985. *Power-Sharing in South Africa*. Policy Papers in International Affairs #24. Berkeley: Institute of International Studies, University of California, Berkeley.

————. 1990a. "Electoral Systems, Party Systems and Conflict Management in Segmented Societies." In *Critical Choices for South Africa: An Agenda for the 1990s*, Robert Schrire, ed. Cape Town, South Africa: Oxford University Press.

————. 1990b. "The Political Consequences of Electoral Laws, 1945–85." *American Political Science Review* 84:481–496.

————. 1991. "The Alternative Vote: A Realistic Alternative for South Africa?" *Politikon* 18(2):91–101.

————. 1994a. *Electoral Systems and Party Systems: A Study of Twenty-Seven Democracies, 1945–1990*. Oxford, U.K.: Oxford University Press.

————. 1994b. *The Puzzle of Indian Democracy: A Reinterpretation*. RGICS Paper No. 18. New Delhi, India: Rajiv Gandhi Institute for Contemporary Studies.

————. 1995. "Self Determination versus Pre-Determination of Ethnic Minorities in Power-sharing Systems." In *The Rights of Minority Cultures*, Will Kymlicka, ed. Oxford, U.K.: Oxford University Press.

Lijphart, Arend, and Bernard Grofman, eds. 1986. *Choosing an Electoral System: Issues and Alternatives*. New York: Praeger.

Linz, Juan J. 1990. "The Perils of Presidentialism." *Journal of Democracy* 1(1):72–84.

Lipset, Seymour Martin. 1960. *Political Man: The Social Bases of Politics*. New York: Doubleday.

————. 1990. "The Centrality of Political Culture." *Journal of Democracy* 1(4):80–83.

Lund, Michael S. 1996. *Preventing Violent Conflicts: A Strategy for Preventive Diplomacy*. Washington, D.C.: United States Institute of Peace Press.

Lustick, Ian. 1979. "Stability in Deeply Divided Societies: Consociationalism versus Control." *World Politics* 31:325–344.

————. 1980. *Arabs in the Jewish State: Israel's Control of a National Minority*. Austin: University of Texas Press.

Maila, Joseph. 1992. *Prospects for Lebanon: The Document of National Understanding*. Oxford, U.K.: Centre for Lebanese Studies.

Maynes, Charles William. 1993. "Containing Ethnic Conflict." *Foreign Policy* 90:3–21.

McRae, Kenneth, ed. 1974. *Consociational Democracy: Political Accommodation in Segmented Societies*. Toronto: McLelland and Stewart.

Meadwell, Hudson. 1989. "Ethnic Nationalism and Collective Choice Theory." *Comparative Political Studies* 22(2):139–154.

———. 1991. "A Rational Choice Approach to Political Regionalism." *Comparative Politics* 23(4):401–422.

Mill, John Stuart. [1861] 1958. *Considerations on Representative Government*. New York: Liberal Arts Press.

Montville, Joseph, ed. 1990. *Conflict and Peacemaking in Multiethnic Societies*. Lexington, Mass.: Lexington Books.

Nariman, Fali Sam. 1989. "The Indian Constitution: An Experiment in Unity Amid Diversity." In *Forging Unity Out of Diversity*, Robert A. Goldwin, Art Kaufman, and William A. Schambra, eds. Washington, D.C.: American Enterprise Institute for Public Policy Research.

Nordlinger, Eric A. 1972. *Conflict Regulation in Divided Societies*. Cambridge, Mass.: Center for International Affairs, Harvard University.

Northrup, Terrell A. 1989. "The Dynamic of Identity in Personal and Social Conflict." In *Intractable Conflicts and Their Resolution*, Louis Kriesberg, Terrell A. Northrup, and Stuart J. Thorson, eds. Syracuse, N.Y.: Syracuse University Press.

O'Donnell, Guillermo, Phillippe C. Schmitter, and Laurence Whitehead. 1986. *Transitions from Authoritarian Rule: Prospects for Democracy*. Baltimore, Md.: Johns Hopkins University Press.

Pappalardo, Adriano. 1981. "The Conditions for Consociational Democracy: A Logical and Empirical Critique." *European Journal of Political Research* 8(4):365–390.

Pillar, Paul R. 1983. *Negotiating Peace: War Termination as a Bargaining Process*. Princeton, N.J.: Princeton University Press.

Posen, Barry. 1993. "The Security Dilemma and Ethnic Conflict." In *Ethnic Conflict and International Security*, Michael Brown, ed. Princeton, N.J.: Princeton University Press.

Przeworski, Adam. 1988. "Democracy as a Contingent Outcome of Conflicts." In *Constitutionalism and Democracy*, Jon Elster and Rune Slagstad, eds. Cambridge, U.K.: Cambridge University Press.

———. 1991. *Democracy and the Market*. Cambridge, U.K.: Cambridge University Press.

Ra'anan, Uri. 1991. "Nation and State: Order Out of Chaos." In *State and Nation in Multi-Ethnic Societies*," Uri Ra'anan, Maria Mesner, Keith Armes, and Kate Martin, eds. Manchester, U.K.: Manchester University Press.

Rabushka, Alvin, and Kenneth A. Shepsle. 1972. *Politics in Plural Societies: A Theory of Democratic Instability.* Columbus, Ohio: Charles E. Merrill.

Rae, Douglas W. 1969. "Decision-Rules and Individual Values in Constitutional Choice." *American Political Science Review* 63:40–56.

Rae, Douglas W., and Michael Taylor. 1970. *The Analysis of Political Cleavages.* New Haven, Conn.: Yale University Press.

Reynolds, Andrew S. Forthcoming. "Re-Running the 1994 South African and Malawi Elections." *Journal of Democracy.*

Robinson, Pearl T. 1995. "New Rules and Uncertain Outcomes: Elections and Party Systems in Africa's Liberalizing Transitions." Paper presented at the United States Institute of Peace symposium, "Elections and Conflict Resolution in Africa," June 9, Washington, D.C.

Rogowski, Ronald. 1985. "Causes and Varieties of Ethnic Nationalism, A Rationalist Account." In *New Nationalisms of the Developed West*, R. Tiryakian and Ronald Rogowski, eds. Boston: Allen & Ulwin.

Rose, Richard. 1990. "Northern Ireland: The Irreducible Conflict." In *Conflict and Peacemaking in Multiethnic Societies*, Joseph Montville, ed. Lexington, Mass.: Lexington Books.

Rothchild, Donald. 1986. "Hegemonial Exchange: An Alternative Model for Managing Conflict in Middle Africa." In *Ethnicity, Politics and Development*, Dennis L. Thompson and Dov Ronen, eds. Boulder, Colo.: Lynne Rienner.

———. 1995. "Bargaining and State Breakdown in Africa." *Nationalism and Ethnic Politics* 1(1):54-72.

Rothchild, Donald, and Michael W. Foley. 1988. "African States and the Politics of Inclusive Coalitions." In *The Precarious Balance: State and Society in Africa*, Donald Rothchild and Naomi Chazan, eds. Boulder, Colo.: Westview Press.

Rothchild, Donald, and Victor Olurunsola, eds. 1986. *State versus Ethnic Claims: African Policy Dilemmas.* Boulder, Colo.: Westview Press.

Rudolph, Joseph R., and Robert J. Thompson. 1989. *Ethnoterritorial Politics, Policy and the Western World.* Boulder, Colo.: Lynne Rienner.

Samarasinghe, S.W. R. de A., and Reed Coughlan. 1991. *Economic Dimensions of Ethnic Conflict.* New York: St. Martin's Press.

Samia, Elie. "The Taif Agreement: Implications for Conflict Resolution in Lebanon." Forthcoming. In *Acknowledgement, Forgiveness and Reconciliation: Lessons from Lebanon*, George Irani and Laurie Kings, eds. Gainsville, Fla.: University Presses of Florida.

Sartori, Giovanni. 1962. "Constitutionalism: A Preliminary Discussion." *American Political Science Review* 56:853–864.

————. 1966. "European Political Parties: The Case of Polarized Pluralism." In *Political Parties and Political Development*, Joseph LaPalombara and Myron Wiener, eds. Princeton, N.J.: Princeton University Press.

————. 1968. "Political Development and Political Engineering." In *Public Policy* No. 17, John D. Montgomery and Alfred O. Hirschmann, eds. Cambridge, Mass.: Harvard University Press.

Saunders, Harold. 1985. "We Need a Larger Theory of Negotiation: The Importance of Pre-Negotiation Phases." *Negotiation Journal* 1(3): 249–262.

Schelling, Thomas. 1960. *The Strategy of Conflict*. Cambridge, Mass.: Harvard University Press.

Share, Donald. 1986. *The Making of Spanish Democracy*. New York: Praeger.

Sisk, Timothy D. 1993a. "Choosing an Electoral System: South Africa Seeks New Ground Rules." *Journal of Democracy* 4(1):79–91.

————. 1993b. "The Violence-Negotiation Nexus: South Africa in Transition and the Politics of Uncertainty." *Negotiation Journal* 9(1):77–94.

————. 1995a. *Democratization in South Africa: The Elusive Social Contract*. Princeton, N.J.: Princeton University Press.

————. 1995b. "Electoral System Choice in South Africa: Implications for Intergroup Moderation." *Nationalism and Ethnic Politics*, 1(2):178–204.

Sklar, Richard. 1985. "Reds and Rights: Zimbabwe's Experiment." *Issue: A Journal of Opinion* 14:29–33.

————. 1987. "Developmental Democracy." *Comparative Studies in Society and History* 29:688–714.

Smith, Anthony. 1981. *The Ethnic Revival in the Modern World*. Cambridge, U.K.: Cambridge University Press.

————. 1993. "The Sources of Ethnic Nationalism." In *Ethnic Conflict and International Security*, Michael Brown, ed. Princeton, N.J.: Princeton University Press.

Smith, M.G. 1965. *The Plural Society in British West Indies*. Berkeley: University of California Press.

Stavenhagen, Rodolfo. 1994. "Reflections on Some Theories of Ethnic Conflict." *Journal of Ethnopolitical Development* 4(1):15–19.

Stedman, Stephen John. 1995. "United Nations Intervention in Civil Wars: Imperatives of Choice and Strategy." In *Beyond Traditional Peacekeeping*, Donald C. Daniel and Bradd C. Hayes, eds. London: Macmillan.

Stein, Janice Gross. 1989. "Getting to the Table: The Triggers, Stages, Functions and Consequences of Prenegotiation." In *Getting to the Table: The Processes of International Prenegotiation*, Janice Gross Stein, ed. Baltimore, Md.: Johns Hopkins University Press.

Steiner, Jurg. 1974. *Amicable Agreement versus Majority Rule: Conflict Resolution in Switzerland*. Chapel Hill, N.C.: University of North Carolina Press.

———. 1981a. "The Consociational Theory and Beyond." *Comparative Politics* 13(April):348–351.

———. 1981b. "Research Strategies Beyond Consociational Theory." *Journal of Politics* (November):1241–1250.

Steinhart, Ralph G. 1994. "International Law and Self-Determination." Occasional Paper of the Atlantic Council of the United States, Washington, D.C.

Suberu, Rotimi. 1994. "The Travails of Federalism in Nigeria." In *Nationalism, Ethnic Conflict, and Democracy*, Larry Diamond and Marc F. Plattner, eds. Baltimore, Md.: Johns Hopkins University Press.

Suhrke, Astri, and L.G. Noble, eds. 1977. *Ethnic Conflict in International Relations*. New York: Praeger.

Taagepera, Rein, and Matthew Soberg Shugart. 1989. *Seats and Votes: The Effects and Determinants of Electoral Systems*. New Haven, Conn.: Yale University Press.

Touval, Saadia. 1994. "Why the UN Fails." *Foreign Affairs* 73(5).

———. 1995. "Ethical Dilemmas in International Mediation." *Negotiation Journal* 11(4):333–338.

Touval, Saadia, and I. William Zartman, eds. 1985. *International Mediation in Theory and Practice*. Boulder, Colo.: Westview Press.

Tsebelis, George. 1990. "Elite Interaction and Constitution Building in Consociational Democracies." *Journal of Theoretical Politics* 2(1):5–29.

Van den Berghe, Pierre. 1981. *The Ethnic Phenomenon*. Oxford, U.K.: Elsevier.

Väyrynen, Raimo, and Janie Leatherman. 1995. "Structure, Culture, and Territory: Three Sets of Early Warning Indicators." Paper presented at the International Studies Association Annual Meeting, Chicago Ill., February 21–25.

Wagner, Robert Harrison. 1993. "The Causes of Peace." In *Stopping the Killing: How Civil Wars End*, Roy Licklider, ed. New York: New York University Press.

Walker, Jenonne. 1993. "International Mediation of Ethnic Conflict." In *Ethnic Conflict and International Security*, Michael Brown, ed. Princeton, N.J.: Princeton University Press.

Walker, Lee, and Paul C. Stern, eds. 1993. *Balancing and Sharing Power in Multiethnic Societies: Summary of a Workshop*. Washington, D.C.: National Academy Press.

Waterman, Harvey. 1993. "Political Order and the 'Settlement' of Civil Wars." In *Stopping the Killing: How Civil Wars End*, Roy Licklider, ed. New York: New York University Press.

Weiss, Thomas G. 1994. "The UN and Civil Wars." *Washington Quarterly* 14(4):139–59.

Welsh, David. 1993. "Domestic Politics and Ethnic Conflict." In *Ethnic Conflict and International Security*, Michael Brown, ed. Princeton, N.J.: Princeton University Press.

Wheare, Sir Kenneth. 1964. *Modern Constitutions*. London: Oxford University Press.

Wolpert, Stanley. 1992. *A History of India*. Oxford, U.K.: Oxford University Press.

Young, Crawford. 1995. "Ethnic Diversity and Public Policy: An Overview." United Nations Institute for Social Development, draft occasional paper.

Zartman, I. William 1991. "Common Elements in the Analysis of a Negotiation Process." In *Negotiation Theory and Practice*, J. William Breslin and Jeffrey Z. Rubin, eds. Cambridge, Mass.: Program on Negotiation, Harvard Law School.

Carnegie Commission on Preventing Deadly Conflict

Carnegie Corporation of New York established the Carnegie Commission on Preventing Deadly Conflict in May 1994 to address the looming threats to world peace of intergroup violence and to advance new ideas for the prevention and resolution of deadly conflict. The Commission is examining the principal causes of deadly ethnic, nationalist, and religious conflicts within and between states and the circumstances that foster or deter their outbreak. Taking a long-term, worldwide view of violent conflicts that are likely to emerge, it is seeking to determine the functional requirements of an effective system for preventing mass violence and to identify the ways in which such a system could be implemented. The Commission is also looking at the strengths and weaknesses of various international entities in conflict prevention and considering ways in which international organizations might contribute toward developing an effective international system of nonviolent problem solving.

Members of the Commission

David A. Hamburg, *Cochair,* President, Carnegie Corporation of New York

Cyrus R. Vance, *Cochair,* Partner, Simpson Thacher & Bartlett

Gro Harlem Brundtland, Prime Minister of Norway

Virendra Dayal, Member, Human Rights Commission of India

Gareth Evans, Former Minister for Foreign Affairs, Government of Australia

Alexander L. George, Graham H. Stuart Professor Emeritus of International Relations, Stanford University

Flora MacDonald, Chair, International Development Research Centre

Donald F. McHenry, University Research Professor of Diplomacy and International Affairs, Georgetown University

Olara A. Otunnu, President, International Peace Academy

David Owen, Chairman, Humanitas

Shridath Ramphal, Cochairman, Commission on Global Governance

Roald Z. Sagdeev, Distinguished Professor, Department of Physics, University of Maryland

John D. Steinbruner, Director, Foreign Policy Studies Program, The Brookings Institution

Brian Urquhart, Scholar-in-Residence, International Affairs Program, The Ford Foundation

John C. Whitehead, Chairman, AEA Investors Inc.

Sahabzada Yaqub-Khan, Special Representative of the United Nations Secretary-General for the Western Sahara

Special Advisor to the Commission
Herbert S. Okun, Executive Director, Financial Services Volunteer Corps

Jane E. Holl, *Executive Director*